SHAKESPEAREAN SYNOPSES

THE LONDON OF SHAKESPEARE'S PLAYS

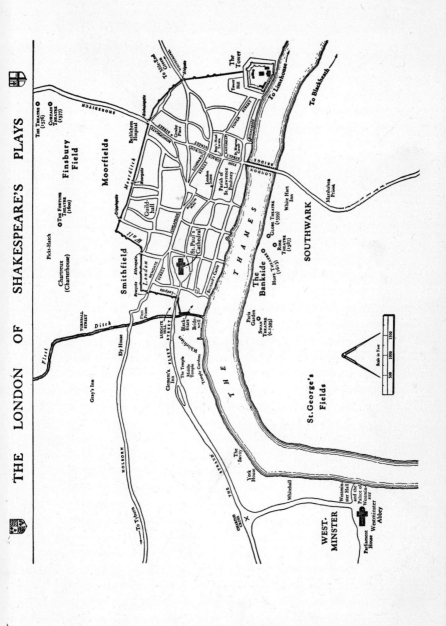

SHAKESPEAREAN SYNOPSES

❧ ❧ ❧

*Outlines of All the Plays
of Shakespeare*

J. WALKER McSPADDEN *Joseph* *1874–*

With an Article on Shakespeare's Stage

BY SUE G. WALCUTT

THOMAS Y. CROWELL COMPANY
New York · Established 1834

The frontispiece map is reproduced from *Selected Plays of Shakespeare* by Holzknecht and McClure, by permission of American Book Company. The plans on pages 10–13 are reproduced from *Shakespeare's Globe Playhouse* by Irwin Smith, copyright © 1956 by Charles Scribner's Sons, by permission of Charles Scribner's Sons and John Cranford Adams.

105092

DESIGNED BY LAUREL WAGNER

*Manufactured in the United States of America
by the Vail-Ballou Press, Inc., Binghamton, New York*

LIBRARY OF CONGRESS CATALOG CARD NUMBER 59-12508

CONTENTS

❀ ❀ ❀

SHAKESPEARE'S STAGE	I
LIFE OF SHAKESPEARE	44
POEMS AND SONNETS	47
CHRONOLOGICAL ORDER OF THE PLAYS	49
THE TEMPEST	51
THE TWO GENTLEMEN OF VERONA	55
THE MERRY WIVES OF WINDSOR	59
MEASURE FOR MEASURE	63
THE COMEDY OF ERRORS	67
MUCH ADO ABOUT NOTHING	71
LOVE'S LABOUR'S LOST	75
A MIDSUMMER NIGHT'S DREAM	79
THE MERCHANT OF VENICE	83
AS YOU LIKE IT	87
THE TAMING OF THE SHREW	91
ALL'S WELL THAT ENDS WELL	95
TWELFTH NIGHT	99
THE WINTER'S TALE	103
CYMBELINE	107
CORIOLANUS	III

viii   CONTENTS

KING JOHN 2369   115

KING RICHARD THE SECOND 2739   119

KING HENRY THE FOURTH PART I 2999   123

KING HENRY THE FOURTH PART II 3094   127

KING HENRY THE FIFTH 3215   131

KING HENRY THE SIXTH PART I 2665   135

KING HENRY THE SIXTH PART II 3094   139

KING HENRY THE SIXTH PART III 2896   143

KING RICHARD THE THIRD 3578   147

KING HENRY THE EIGHTH 2809   151

TROILUS AND CRESSIDA 3342   155

TITUS ANDRONICUS 2614   159

ROMEO AND JULIET 2983   163

TIMON OF ATHENS 2335   167

JULIUS CÆSAR 2422   171

MACBETH 2085   175

HAMLET 3777   179

KING LEAR 3102   183

OTHELLO 3202   187

ANTONY AND CLEOPATRA 3024   191

PERICLES 2357   195

INDEX TO CHARACTERS   201

SHAKESPEAREAN SYNOPSES

SHAKESPEARE'S STAGE

In the English-speaking world it would be difficult to find a literary name as universally known, among the ignorant as well as the learned, as that of William Shakespeare. If anyone doubts the truth of this statement, let him try registering under that signature at any hotel. A number of years ago a man whose name was, indeed, William Shakespeare, published in a popular magazine an account of the difficulties involved in possessing such a name. Desk clerks took one look at the register and motioned for the house detective; policemen muttered, "Wise guy, huh?" and threatened to run him in; wags replied, "So you're William Shakespeare. Well, I'm Queen Elizabeth."

In spite of the fact that the Bard of Avon was so indifferent to spelling that the six surviving signatures known to be genuine are spelled two different ways, the name William Shakespeare belongs to him and to him alone, and let others use it at their peril—and possible grave inconvenience. It is therefore peculiarly ironical that the works of Shakespeare have not always remained his and his alone—at least not to everyone. For decades there have been scholars and crackpots who have convinced themselves, and by various ingenious means tried to convince others, that the poems and plays of William Shakespeare were written by somebody else: Francis Bacon, Edward de Vere, Christopher Marlowe, or, as Mark Twain suggested, another fellow by the same name. There is some kind of magic about Shakespeare that attracts the greatest minds of all ages, and the silliest. Shakespearean criticism, as a result, is a hodgepodge of brilliant and penetrating theories and appalling imbecilities.

So little is known of Shakespeare the man, and of that little

I

so much is irrelevant to his literary career, that it is no wonder the fabricators have for years been busy weaving legends to cover those bare bones of fact. A great deal is known, however, about life in Shakespeare's times, about Shakespeare's theaters, actors, audiences, staging, music, and even costumes and properties; and every year, as scholars study old records, more information is turned up.

The drama during Shakespeare's lifetime was, like almost everything else in Elizabethan times, in a state of transition and expansion. During the Middle Ages companies of players were attached to noble houses or to the court; they had the status of servants and served by entertaining. Lords and ladies indulged in amateur theatricals themselves, particularly at Christmas time. In addition, boys in schools and universities acted in classical plays as a means, it was said, of acquiring a fluency in Latin as well as a familiarity with the ancient dramatists.

These pleasures were for the aristocratic and the educated, but there was all manner of entertainment for the common people. There were strolling acrobats, ballad singers, jugglers, dancers, and puppeteers. There were also the barbers who cured a toothache by "drawing" the tooth in the market square where the passing idler could amuse himself by listening to the cries and groans of the patient; and, even more fantastic, there were the quacks who cured by strange means even stranger diseases. A prevalent disorder from which the man of the Elizabethan age suffered was a serpent in the belly, a gnawing at his vitals. The quack cured this malady by hoisting the victim upside down on a framework designed for the purpose and placing under his suspended head a saucer of milk. As everyone in medieval times knew, a serpent is unable to resist a drink of milk. Presently the "stomach-snake" would crawl out of the patient's mouth and the triumphant quack, an expert in sleight of hand, would display it to victim and audience alike.

Far more important than these street shows were the religious dramas: the miracle and morality plays. They started originally inside the churches and cathedrals as "living pictures" to illustrate the Bible stories to the congregations who did not understand the Latin of the church service. At Christmas and Easter the "pictures" grew into little dramas. On Good Friday, for example, the Crucifix, representing the dead Christ, was laid in a tomb, and on Easter morning it was resurrected. Monks or choir boys played the parts of the three Marys and the Angel at the tomb while other choir boys took the parts of angels on high, singing in chorus. Soon the number of worshippers became so great that the playlets were moved out into the churchyard or courtyard before the cathedral and, when the audience outgrew this limited space, the plays were transferred to the village green or common. Gradually the production of the "mysteries" or miracle plays became too complicated for the priests and monks, who had more serious duties to perform, and was taken over by the guilds. Each guild specialized in some particular subject most appropriate to it: the ship carpenters' guild presented the play of Noah and the Ark; the bakers', the Last Supper; the butchers', the Crucifixion; and each guild tried to surpass the others.

At the height of their popularity, there was such a demand for the miracle plays that performances were repeated in different parts of town until everyone had a chance to see them. The plays were presented on wooden platforms mounted on wheels. These little movable theaters were two stories high: the upper part was the wooden stage on which the play was given; the lower story served both as a dressing or "tiring" room and as an entrance to "hell." On the front was painted a "hell mouth," a pair of enormous jaws, out of which leaped red devils with horrible false heads and pitchforks, and into which were dragged, shrieking, the lost souls. Smoke, flames, and the howls of tormented sinners poured out of the red jaws of hell.

Since the way in which the miracle plays were produced exerted considerable influence on the Shakespearean theater, it is worth having a look at the events that took place on Corpus Christi day, usually in the first week of June, in a provincial town in England—Chester, perhaps, or York. Early in the morning a crier, announcing the production, went about the town, and long before curtain time the audience had assembled, standing in the street, occupying tiers of temporary wooden seats, or looking out from the windows and balconies of nearby houses. The "pageant" or play-wagon lumbered in, pulled by apprentices of the guild in charge of the play. When the curtains around the outside of the stage were drawn, all four sides were exposed to the audience.

The play might deal with the fall of Lucifer, the Creation, or any event in the Old Testament or in the life of Christ. The present-day British taboo against presenting the deity as a character on the stage would have struck a medieval audience as preposterous; God was an essential player. He sat on a raised throne, wearing a red robe and gilded hair and beard. A number of the characters of the miracle plays wore conventional costumes by which the audience recognized them instantly. Angels had gilded wings and hair, devils wore false heads, Herod always dressed as a Saracen in a gorgeous turban, and kings always wore crowns. (This last convention was observed by Shakespeare.)

An important stage device was the trap door set in the floor of the upper stage, from which devils and spirits from hell could emerge on stage. Other irrelevant devils contributed comic effects by rushing out of the "hell mouth," which was on a level with the audience, and engaging in such horseplay as menacing the spectators with pitchforks and threatening to drag them off to hell. If they were to appear on the stage, however, they usually came up through the trap door.

The trap was also occasionally used for other surprise effects. In the play about the Creation, for example, the curtain parted to reveal God the Creator on his throne, with Adam, newly created, lying at his feet, dressed in a tight-fitting leather suit painted white or flesh-color to represent nakedness. When God, announcing that he was going to create Eve, touched Adam's side, the trap door opened, perhaps veiled or "masked" from most of the audience by God's voluminous robe, and Eve magically appeared.

Many of the customs and procedures of the miracle players were taken up by the roving bands of players in pre-Shakespearean England. During the sixteenth century, players were associated with royal or noble households, but the earliest companies seem to have been unattached. In 1427, "interludes" were performed before Henry VI by the Players of Abington, apparently a town troupe. There are records between 1492 and 1509 of town players from Wymborne, Minster, London, and Mile End performing at court. Many acting companies were stationary, made up of town craftsmen and artisans, or of groups of servants from the great houses. Peter Quince's company of players in *A Midsummer Night's Dream,* composed of a carpenter, a weaver, a bellows maker, a tinker, a joiner, and a tailor, was by no means unusual. Some actors were displaced priests, students who had failed at the universities, singing boys who had outgrown their ability to sing—in short, almost anyone except a member of the upper classes might become a professional actor.

When the troupes wanted to travel around the country giving performances, they needed credentials from a nobleman, but these were easily obtained. The companies took the name of the nobleman who licensed them, and became known as "Essex's Men" or "Norfolk's Men" or Companies, but the connection was a loose one. The lord for whom the company was named was not a patron in the modern sense of supporting the troupe. Some companies walked from village to village with their properties on their backs or upon a single pack animal; others traveled in wagons. Sometimes in their wanderings they might play at a manor house or castle where the owner would be so beguiled by their acting that he would house them for months or even years. The earliest companies were composed of four men, the smallest among them taking the women's parts; sometimes a boy traveled with them as an apprentice, but it was not until well along in the sixteenth century that "his Ladyship," the boy who starred in the women's parts, was added. Between 1494 and 1552 the companies grew from four to eight members; from 1576 to 1577 there are records of troupes varying in numbers from six to twelve.

Without a theater of their own, the actors, when not playing in private houses, gave their performances in public squares, village greens, barns, town halls, schoolhouses, and innyards.

The innyards were especially convenient, since they consisted of large open courts with galleries. The players erected a make-shift platform, set on barrelheads, and the nearby stables were used as dressing rooms. The ordinary playgoers, the vast and motley "poor," stood pressed around the stage, almost at a level with it; the more aristocratic spectators were seated comfortably in the galleries above.

Like the old-fashioned circuses of forty years ago, the plays were advertised by a parade: a drummer and a trumpeter marched about the street collecting followers like the Pied Piper. Sober people disapproved of the racket, particularly the loud voice of the trumpet; sometimes the musician was molested and occasionally he was arrested. But the common people loved the stirring notes and followed joyfully after them. When the crowd had grown to satisfactory proportions, one of the musicians announced the time and place of the performance. Playbills or posters were put up in prominent spots to make the same announcements, but, because so many people were illiterate, the drum-and-trumpet parade was a much more effective advertisement. Shakespeare refers to the practice of drumming up business in Act IV, scene 3, of *All's Well That Ends Well*. The First Soldier inquires, "What say you of his expertness in war?" and receives the reply, "Faith, sir, he has led the drum before the English tragedians"; in other words, his experience in warfare has been limited to drumming for the players, either before the play, or in battle scenes, or both.

Such an informal means of advertisement worked well enough in the small towns, but in the city of London it was hardly an adequate method of attracting an audience, nor were the idlers of London the "best people," and as the city players became wealthier and more serious about their pro-fession, they naturally wanted a more elevated audience. Gradually, in answer to the demand, certain innkeepers, whether because such a venture was profitable or because, like some "angels" today, they found the enchantment of the theater pay enough, slighted their ordinary business and made show business their primary concern. They erected permanent stages in their yards, installed wooden benches in the galleries, and allowed the theatrical troupes to use the buildings in exchange for a share in the box-office receipts. With this convenient arrangement, the actors could always be sure of a theater and the public knew where it could always go to find entertainment.

But when has play production, or, for that matter, play-going, ever had smooth sailing? No sooner had the actors found a place of their own than their enemies contrived to render them homeless again. On December 6, 1574, an Order of the Common Council was issued, forbidding innkeepers, tavern keepers, or anyone else to "openly show, or play, within the houseyard or any other place" within the city proper any play whatever. The Puritans believed that the Bible expressly forbade play-acting, or perhaps they read Holy Writ in such a way as to find this stricture, for they were constitutionally opposed to most forms of amusement. "The Puritans," said Macaulay, "hated bear-baiting, not because it gave pain to the bear, but because it gave pleasure to the spectators." They waged a constant war against the theater, and the playwrights counterattacked with their deadliest weapon—ridicule. Some of the attacks were coarse and scurrilous; but Shakespeare, whose taste and temper were better than his contemporaries', poked good-natured fun at the Puritans in *Twelfth Night*. Malvolio, in Act II, scene 3, is taunted by Sir Toby and the Clown for his puritanical beliefs in the following often quoted lines:

SIR TOBY. Dost thou think, because thou art virtuous, there shall be no more cakes and ale?
CLOWN. Yes, by Saint Anne, and ginger hot i' the mouth too.

The Puritans were aided in their effort to stamp out the theater by the city fathers of London, whose objections were practical rather than religious, and by a third group, for a still different reason, but these objections will be discussed later.

How many inns and taverns were affected by the law against the players is not known, although at least five large inns had companies of actors attached to them. But human nature is ever resourceful in circumventing unpleasant and unpopular laws and, under the pretext of "rehearsing" their plays for private production, some companies managed to perform within the city limits, even though there was always the danger that the actors might be arrested and carried off to jail.

In 1576 something happened that may well have changed the course of the English theater. James Burbage, a member of the Earl of Leicester's Company, tired, perhaps, of being chivvied about, decided to build the first permanent playhouse in London. He chose a site in Shoreditch, a suburb north of London, on land leased from Giles Alleyn. Burbage was excellently qualified for his rôle of pioneer playhouse builder. As a former actor, he knew what was needed for the stage and the stage machinery; as the manager of a highly successful company of actors, he knew how the galleries and passages in the theater could best be arranged for the convenience of the audience and the money-takers alike. He had been trained as a carpenter, he had a natural gift for design, and he was courageous and imaginative enough to attempt something that had never been done before.

Although it is generally believed that the Theatre, as it was called, was patterned upon the innyard, the shape was modified, probably influenced by the bearbaiting rings, although some scholars think that the classical amphitheaters also influenced the shape. At any rate, instead of preserving the rectangle of the innyards, the Theatre was octagonal.

It would be pleasant to be able to report that Burbage's courage and enterprise were rewarded by success and prosperity, but such is far from the case. The Theatre was beset by so much trouble that the superstitious might well believe it was jinxed. Burbage's partner and brother-in-law, Brayne, brought him nothing but grief, litigation, and debts; but an even greater stumbling block was his landlord, who always promised to renew the lease, but constantly put off doing so.

James Burbage died two months before the lease expired, leaving the Theatre to his son Cuthbert, who tried to have the lease extended, only to be thwarted, like his father, by evasions and procrastinations. He therefore decided that the time had come for drastic action. Since it was impossible to pin Giles Alleyn down on whether he would renew the lease, Cuthbert resolved to build a new theater out of whatever timbers he could salvage from the old. His contract stated that, provided he moved it before the lease expired, the material of the theater was his.

In order to finance the purchase of a building site and the construction of the new theater, Cuthbert formed a syndicate composed of his younger brother Richard and five other leading actors of the Lord Chamberlain's Company, including William Shakespeare, already a successful playwright, and William Kempe, the finest comedian of his day.

The site chosen for the new playhouse was on the far side of the river, near London Bridge, in an area known as Southwark on the Bankside, outside the city limits. The section was not one that had the best possible reputation; it was the location of the brothels and the Bear Garden, so hated by the Puritans. Still, the Puritans were not going to be reconciled to the theater, no matter how respectable its neighborhood, and Bankside had a number of advantages. It was outside the jurisdiction of the Common Council, it was easily accessible to the public by bridge or ferry, and the banner that was flown to indicate that a performance was to take place on that day could be seen from the other side of the Thames, where the theatergoers lived. There were already two theaters on Bankside, the Swan, built in 1594, and the Rose, built by Philip Henslowe, probably about 1587, and remodeled in 1592. It was then occupied by Lord Strange's Men (later known as the Lord Chamberlain's Company, with which Shakespeare was identified) with Edward Alleyn at the head. Possibly the best actors in London, Lord Strange's Men opened the refurbished theater on February 19, 1592, with a performance of Robert Greene's *Friar Bacon and Friar Bungay*. Other important plays given at the Rose include *The Spanish Tragedy* by Kyd, *The Jew of Malta* by Marlowe, and *Henry VI* by Shakespeare. Early in 1594, while Strange's Men were on a long country tour, Sussex's Men performed *Titus Andronicus* at the Rose; and on

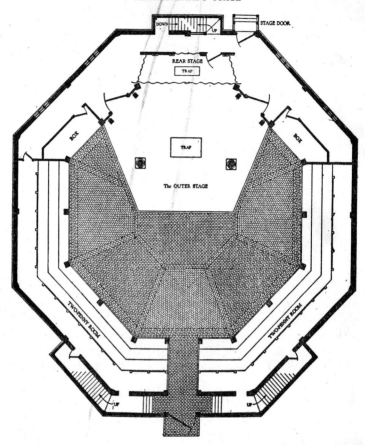

THE GLOBE PLAYHOUSE

SCALE DRAWING I   **FLOOR PLAN AT FIRST LEVEL**

April 1, 1594, the Queen's Men and Sussex's Men together presented *King Lear*. No documentary proof exists that Shakespeare ever acted in this theater, although it is possible that he did. When the Globe opened in the summer of 1599 it far outshone both its neighbors. Much admired by the theater world, it was referred to by Ben Jonson as "this fair-fitted Globe," and "the glory of the Banke."

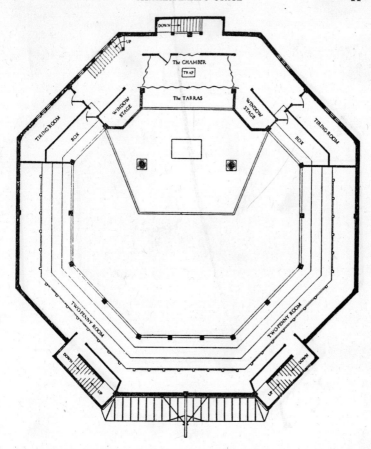

THE GLOBE PLAYHOUSE

SCALE DRAWING II   **FLOOR PLAN AT SECOND LEVEL**

Unlike the troubled Theatre, the Globe seems to have run into no legal difficulties whatsoever. The seven men who made up the original syndicate continued as owners and proprietors of the new playhouse, and were called in their day "house-keepers." The attached troupe of actors, known as the "company," owned the costumes, properties, and playbooks, and were responsible for casting, rehearsing, and producing the

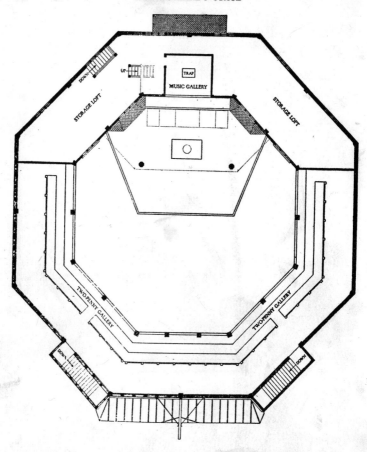

THE GLOBE PLAYHOUSE

SCALE DRAWING III   **FLOOR PLAN AT THIRD LEVEL**

plays. They had a share in the box-office receipts. It is not necessary here to go any further into the financial organization except to add that it worked extremely well. It was his share in the Globe rather than his earnings as a dramatist that made Shakespeare's fortune and enabled him to retire to the peace and quiet of Stratford, one of the wealthiest men in the town.

It is true, however, that a portion of Shakespeare's wealth

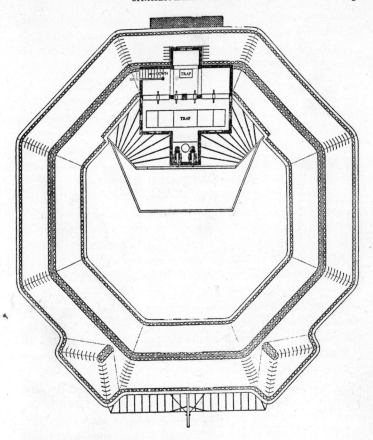

THE GLOBE PLAYHOUSE

SCALE DRAWING IV   **PLAN AT SUPERSTRUCTURE LEVEL**

came from his part ownership of Blackfriars theater, formerly
a monastery. Richard Burbage bought it in 1597, leasing it for
the next ten years to a company of boy actors who rapidly became famous. They were so talented that they gave their elders
stiff competition. It is to these gifted children (the Children
of the Chapel) that Shakespeare alludes in *Hamlet,* Act II,
scene 2:

ROSENCRANTZ. . . . there is, sir, an aery of children, little eyases, that cry out on the top of question, and are most tyrannically clapped for 't: these are now the fashion, and so berattle the common stages,—so they call them,—that many wearing rapiers are afraid of goose-quills, and dare scarce come hither.

In 1608 or 1609, after the lease had expired, Shakespeare's company put on plays there as well as in the Globe. Blackfriars was an indoor theater and, if it was more expensive, it was also more comfortable. It was doubtless used as a winter theater while the Globe served during the milder months.

Today, because of the Sir Laurence Olivier film of *Henry V,* with its prologue showing the Globe theater, and because of the beautifully made replicas at Stratford, Ontario, and at Stratford, Connecticut, thousands of Americans are familiar with the more obvious aspects of the Globe. Only a few of them realize how little is actually known about the first Globe, what years of painful searching through old records have been spent to assemble details about the building, and how much of the construction is based upon conjecture. No one today knows *exactly* what the Globe looked like in Shakespeare's day, and the scholars who know the most do not always agree.

The exact location of the Globe has been a matter of great interest to Shakespearean historians. There are a number of contemporary maps of London showing the theaters, but they hardly solve the problem, since one map puts the Globe in one place, another map in a different spot. One map may show the theaters, but it is impossible to tell which is the Globe, which the Rose or the Swan. The map which most scholars agree is most likely to be correct, made in 1600, shows the Globe at an angle formed by two drainage ditches, one on the south side of Maid (or Maiden) Lane, one on the southeast side. Maiden Lane is described in Stryke's 1720 edition of Stowe's earlier *Survey of London* as follows: "Maiden Lane, a long straggling place, with ditches on each side, the passages to the houses being over little bridges, with little garden plots before them, especially on the north side, which is best both for houses and inhabitants." Ben Jonson in his poem "An Execration Upon Vulcan" mentions the Globe as being "Flanck'd by a Ditch, and forc'd out of a Marish [marsh]."

The London County Council's *Survey of London* puts the Globe on the site of the Anchor Brewery, which belonged in the eighteenth century to Henry Thrale, the husband of Dr. Samuel Johnson's landlady and friend. In her memoirs Mrs. Thrale writes:

> For a long time, then—or I thought it such—my fate was bound up with the old Globe Theatre, upon the Bankside, Southwork; the alley it had occupied having been purchased and thrown down by Mr. Thrale to make an opening before the windows of our dwelling-house. When it lay desolate in a black heap of rubbish, my Mother, one day, in a joke, called it the Ruins of Palmyra; and after that they laid it down in a grass-plot. Palmyra was the name it went by, I suppose, among the clerks and servants of the brewhouse. . . . But there were curious remains of the old Globe Playhouse, which though hexagonal in form without, was round within.

Although later investigations have determined that the original site of the Globe was more to the north, Mrs. Thrale was nearly right (as she often was) and if she believed she had seen "curious remains" hexagonal without and round within, she may merely have been embellishing memory with imagination (as she often did) and was no more fanciful than many another Shakespearean historian. The Shakespearean Reading Society put up a tablet on the wall of the Anchor Brewery, and if, like Mrs. Thrale's site, it is not precisely the correct spot, it is within shouting distance.

Interest in reconstructing the Shakespearean theater is of fairly modern date. For a while after the age of Shakespeare, the plays, or at least many of them, were out-of-date, good material for "more gifted writers" to find ideas in for their own plays or operas, but of little interest as they stood. The way in which they were presented was of even less concern to a generation of theatergoers taken up with the elaborate settings that came in with the Restoration. There was no interest at all in Shakespearean playhouses until nearly the end of the eighteenth century when Edmund Malone published an account of the Elizabethan theater, which, though an honest attempt to reconstruct the past, was misleading and inaccurate in many ways.

Shakespeare's prologue to *Henry V* was considered one very important source of information concerning the construction of a playhouse:

> But pardon, gentles all,
> The flat unraised spirits that have dared
> On this unworthy scaffold to bring forth
> So great an object: can this cockpit hold
> The vasty fields of France? or may we cram
> Within the wooden O the very casques
> That did affright the air at Agincourt?
> O, pardon! since a crooked figure may
> Attest in little space a million;
> And let us, ciphers to this great accompt,
> On your imaginary forces work.

and was taken as a literal account of the Globe. Scholars today are by no means agreed that such is the case. One argues that Shakespeare must have meant the Curtain theater, since he speaks of "this unworthy scaffold" and its limitations.* If he had referred to "the glory of the Bank" would these lines have been so modest? Another critic suggests the poet was not speaking of the Globe in particular, but of the Elizabethan theater in general. The "wooden O" has been taken by some as proof that the Globe was circular, while others argued that Shakespeare never intended to be taken literally; moreover, if the theater was hexagonal or twelve- or sixteen-sided, as some believe, the line would have been sadly limping if it had read "within this wooden hexagon." Fortunately the shape makes little difference; whether round or hexagonal, twelve- or sixteen-sided, the Globe was roundish, as the name implies.

It was built in part out of the heavy oak timbers salvaged from the old Theatre. Scholars have made elaborate studies

---

* The Curtain Theater was built in 1577 and derived its name from the Curtain Estate where it stood. The estate was so-called possibly because of some early associations with city walls (curtains) or perhaps from a corruption of *cortina,* medieval Latin for a court or farm enclosure. It had no connection with a stage curtain.

of old English carpenters' marks and of methods of construction, and it is very tempting to go into these details, if only because of the quaint names attached—prick-posts, dragon beams (a corruption of "diagonal"), breastsummers, and binding joists. But it is enough to know that the exterior of the Globe was made of the plaster-and-oak construction that one associates with Elizabethan half-timbering. Unlike today's imitation black-and-white Tudor veneer, the material was not chosen for its picturesque quality, but because it was an effective and inexpensive construction. The great oak timbers were filled between by a wattle-and-daub construction; that is, a kind of basketwork made of unpeeled hazel wands which was plastered on both sides with clay or loam mixed with hair or straw, and whitewashed on the outside to seal and protect it from the weather. The galleries running around the open court were thatched, as was the main roof over the covered part of the stage, but there were smaller, secondary roofs over other parts that were probably tiled.

Such was the outside appearance of the Globe, a round or many-sided structure of gleaming white plaster and old oak beams, with covered galleries and at one end a cluster of small peaked roofs over which the bright banner flew to announce the presentation of a play.

' Although a few descriptions of London theaters were written by foreign travelers, before 1888 only three small contemporary pictures of the sixteenth- and seventeenth-century stage were known. They were not very well drawn, it was impossible to tell whether they represented any specific playhouse, and they were all quite different. Scholars, however, spent a great deal of time poring over them.

In 1888 a sketch of the interior of the Swan theater (which was thought to be not very dissimilar from the Globe) was found by a German critic in the university library at Utrecht, along with other memoranda of Johannes DeWitt, who visited London in 1596. The drawing was made not by DeWitt himself, but by his friend Arend van Buchell, and it has been described disparagingly by Dover Wilson as "one Dutchman's copy of another Dutchman's sketch of what he remembered about the interior of the Swan Theatre after a single visit." Crude though it is, it shows a number of interesting details, such as the proscenium, or platform stage, supported on what look like tree stumps or barrelheads, and jutting far out into the pit, with a space, apparently, on three sides for the "groundlings" to stand. It shows the "ingressus" or door into the pit, the place for the musicians, the inner stage with its two doors, the gallery above with figures on it, the "hut" above that, and the silken banner fluttering over all. It is puzzling that the curtains of the inner stage are not indicated, but it is possible that DeWitt simply forgot about them, since it is natural to think of the stage with the curtains parted. It is certainly not much of a picture; it is ill-drawn and doubtless inaccurate, but it is, as Sir Edmund K. Chambers, the great authority on Shakespearean theaters, says, "the inevitable basis of any comprehensive account of the main structural features of the playhouse."

The question of the height of the platform or outer stage has been a source of disagreement among scholars. DeWitt's sketch suggests that it was four or five feet above the floor of the pit. The observations of Thomas Platter of Basle who in 1599 wrote the following account of the London theaters support DeWitt's sketch: "The playhouses are so constructed that they play on a raised platform, so that everyone has a good view. There are different galleries and places, however, where the seating is better and more comfortable and therefore more expensive. For whoever cares to stand below pays one English penny, but if he wishes to sit he enters by another door, and pays another penny, while if he wishes to sit in the most comfortable seats which are cushioned, where he not only sees everything but can also be seen, then he pays yet another English penny at another door."

The playgoer entered the theater through a little door over which hung a signboard decorated, William Malone writes, on information from William Oldys (1696–1761), with "a figure of Hercules supporting the Globe, under which was written *'Totus mundus agit histrionem.'*" * He dropped his penny

* Some scholars dispute this point, claiming that the signboard hung somewhere else, but they do not agree on the exact spot.

into a box held by the doorkeeper, or "gatherer," and was admitted to the open pit of the theater, which was probably paved with bricks or stone. He then had the choice of standing in the pit with the other groundlings, or paying another penny and taking his place on a bench (or perhaps still standing, if the play was a popular one) under the roof of the gallery. Perhaps if he wished to be seen as well as to see he would pay another penny to be admitted to the boxes or part of the gallery nearest the inner stage, although some scholars think that Thomas Platter was referring to the practice, which we know existed, of sitting on the stage itself.

The outer stage of the Globe may have been rectangular, or may have been tapered toward the front; some critics believe it may have been as wide as twenty-four feet, with an area of perhaps 942 square feet, a very large stage even by modern standards. Around the edge was a low balustrade, possibly to keep the groundlings off the stage, and underneath was the cellar or "hell." The presence of the "hell" at the Globe has some bearing on the disputed height of the platform. If it were, as DeWitt and Thomas Platter say, raised a reasonable distance above the pit, then there would be no need for an excavation of more than a foot or two in depth; and if one bears in mind the marshy ground on which the theater was constructed, and the drainage ditches near by, one can easily see that the "hell" would have been a watery rather than a fiery one unless the platform was a few feet above the pit. Whatever the height, the balustrade around the stage must have been something of a nuisance, except to the fashionable spectators seated on the stage, who could use it for a back rest. In *Henry VIII,* Act I, scene 4, there is believed to be an allusion to the balustrade in the speech of the porter, attempting to restrain a crowd of citizens as he clears a path for a procession: "You i' th' chamblet, Get up o' th' rail. I'll peck you o'er the pales else!"

There was a trap, or trap door in the outer stage, leading down into the cellar, an inheritance from the miracle plays; from this trap supernatural spirits and devils appeared. Behind the stage was the elaborate front of the "tiring" house or room. This was originally simply a place for actors to dress, as the name signifies, but in the Shakespearean theater it had become much more than that. It was the dressing room, the back stage, and the stairways and passages up to the various levels. At least one critic has made much of these stairs and passages, attempting to show that they influenced the length of the speeches in Shakespeare's plays. If, for example, an actor was supposed to appear in an upper room for the next scene, another actor would need a speech of, say, twenty lines, to allow the first one enough time to reach his destination. It is hardly necessary to go into this ingenious theory except to point out that in Shakespeare's time there were no intervals between the scenes. The action moved rapidly from one scene to the next, and the fact that there were many different places for the action to take place was an important one in keeping the play moving.

In front of the tiring room was the inner stage, or perhaps it should be called inner stages, since there were at least two and possibly three different levels or stages. The front of the tiring room could be used for the scenery of the inner stages. It may have been painted, as some critics believe, to represent a street scene. The large, substantial doors into the tiring room served not only to keep out the cold of the open courtyard, but were used for scenery. As any thoughtful reader of Shakespeare will notice, there are a number of scenes that take place before gates or doors, doors that are hammered on (sometimes from both sides), unlocked with a key, battered, forced open, and therefore need to be substantial. It has been suggested that the existence of the doors into the tiring room influenced Shakespeare to write these scenes as he did. Frequently in the historical plays they appear as gates to a city; in *Henry IV,* Part I, Act I, scene 3, they are the gates of London; in *Henry VI,* Part III, Act IV, scene 7, of York; in *King John,* Act III, scene 2, of Angiers. In *Romeo and Juliet,* Act V, scene 3, they represent the burial vault of the Capulet family. When gates were not needed, and the inner stage was supposed to represent a room, curtains were hung over the doors.

It must not be forgotten that the inner stage was two or

three stories high, each story having its separate set of curtains that were not raised and lowered, like modern ones, but drawn aside, probably mechanically, with cords and pulleys, although some critics think liveried attendants drew them. The third level of the inner stage was a balcony, sometimes used by the actors as a battlement, sometimes by stage musicians, and occasionally, perhaps, by spectators.

Shakespeare wrote a number of scenes which were supposed to take place at some high point, battlements, towers, or the beetling cliffs of Dover, and stage historians are not in agreement about where these scenes were acted. They might have been performed on the third level, but there are writers who believe that they took place on a long shallow balcony projecting out in front of the second-level inner stage. In *Henry VI*, Part I, there are a number of scenes on top of city walls; the walls of Orleans in Acts I and II, Bordeaux in Act IV, and in Act V the scene in Reignier's castle at Angiers is believed to have been played on a high balcony. When Brutus and Mark Antony address the people of Rome from a public pulpit in *Julius Caesar*, they may have done so from the second-level balcony, rather than the third. It has been suggested that it served as a hill in the same play and that in *The Tempest* it was used to represent the quarter-deck of Alonso's ship in Act I, scene 2.

Because battles were fought on this balcony during some of the early historical plays, the second-level balcony was sturdily built, with a balustrade or parapet in front. When the upper inner stage behind it was used, the balustrade would have seriously interfered with the groundlings' view of the action. Irwin Smith, one of the outstanding authorities on the Globe, suggests that in the early plays the upper inner stage had not yet come into use, and that later, when it was utilized for the "chamber," the heavy balustrade was taken out and replaced by slender, widely spaced posts, or even by removable ones.

The upper inner stage, usually referred to as "the chamber," is a hotly disputed subject among stage historians. Although most of them agree that it existed, the extent to which it was used in Shakespearean play productions is endlessly discussed and debated. Some critics believe that some of the most important scenes took place here: Juliet's interview with her father and her drinking of the potion; Hamlet's scene with his mother in her "closet"; here, too, Gloucester's eyes were put out, and here the merry scene in Part II of *Henry IV*, Act II, scene 4, supposedly in "an upper room of the Boar's Head Tavern," is believed to have taken place. There are a number of points in favor of such an arrangement. The use of the chamber would enhance the intimacy of the first two scenes. In the scene of Gloucester's blinding, *King Lear*, Act III, scene 7, the horror and brutality of the action would be reduced a little by the distance.

On the other hand, what Elizabethan audience ever recoiled from bloodshed and cruelty? These were the same people who attended public executions and relished the agony of the mistreated bulls and bears in the pits. Moreover, it would be a pity if one of the most rollicking and boisterous scenes in any comedy, the antics of Falstaff and his friends, were played on a small, distant place. Arguments have been advanced, however, that the upper inner stage was not so far removed; in fact, from the gallery it would have been nearer than the platform stage below, and the gallants there had, after all, paid an extra penny and were therefore entitled to a better view.

Not only did the Globe theater possess a large outer stage, an inner lower stage, an inner upper stage with a balcony extending out from it, and, on the third level, according to a number of critics, a musicians' gallery, but it had in addition a pair of "window stages," one on each side of the inner stage. They were bay windows, swelling out from the supporting wall of the tiring house, with casements, probably opening out rather than in, although this detail, too, has been argued. Tudor windows were small, diamond-shaped pieces of glass that were usually colored and not very transparent, set in a frame of lead, or "leads," as it was generally called. They admitted a pale, subdued light and it was difficult to see through them; an actor behind a window would be a dim figure. The casements would have to be open during any window scene, unless, as one scholar suggests, a set of leads without any glass between could be substituted for the actual window.

In spite of the fact that one of the most famous of all Shakespearean scenes, scene 5, Act III of *Romeo and Juliet,* is popularly referred to as the balcony scene, it was at one of the window stages that young Juliet (the part played by a boy in Shakespeare's day) stood to deliver her beautiful lines:

> Wilt thou be gone? it is not yet near day.
> It was the nightingale, and not the lark,
> That pierc'd the fearful hollow of thine ear.
> Nightly she sings on yond pomegranate tree:
> Believe me, love, it was the nightingale.

and heard Romeo reply:

> It was the lark, the herald of the morn;
> No nightingale. Look, love, what envious streaks
> Do lace the severing clouds in yonder East:
> Night's candles are burnt out, and jocund day
> Stands tiptoe on the misty mountain tops.
> I must be gone and live, or stay and die.

There were, it is easy to see, a number of different places where scenes could take place, at least half a dozen, not counting the outer stage, which alone could be used for several different scenes. In *Richard III,* Act V, scene 3, the platform stage seems to have been used to represent six or seven different places: several parts of Bosworth Field as well as scenes inside and outside of Richard's tent. It is possible, however, that the scene inside the tent was played on the lower inner stage, with the stage curtains representing the open tent flap.

It must not be forgotten that the outer stage was without curtains and was surrounded on three sides by the audience. It was used to represent outdoor scenes such as the Forest of Arden, or the heath in *King Lear,* and for indoor scenes that required considerable space; a scene at court, for example, where there was pomp and ceremony and a large number of actors were present. Although a skirmish in a battle where only

two actors were involved might take place on the upper
balcony, it was usual for fighting and fencing to be carried on
below, where there was plenty of space for the actors to display
their skill.

Any modern theatergoer can see at once the advantages of
the inner stage. The curtains, for one thing, were very lux-
uriant, made of a rich, heavy fabric that lent grandeur to the
scene, delighted the spectators, and added fuel to the fire of
the Puritans' wrath, which always blazed against any display
of "wanton luxury." The curtains could be drawn aside to
reveal ("discover" was the word the Elizabethans used) a
scene already set, as in *The Tempest,* Act V, scene 1, "Here
Prospero discovers Ferdinand and Miranda playing at chess."
They could be drawn together to denote a change of scene
or the passage of time, or to allow the stagehands to remove
properties and substitute other ones. Most important of all, if
a character was supposed to be killed on the inner stage,
there was no need to carry off his body. The inner stages,
furthermore, were sheltered from the weather.

In the Globe theater, it is believed that posts extended from
the inner stage up to the beams, which in turn supported
a wooden superstructure known as the "shadow" or "the
heavens." According to Malone, this stage cover was painted
or decorated: "It was probably painted a sky blue colour,
or perhaps pieces of drapery tinged with blue were suspended
across the stage to represent the heavens." Most scholars accept
the first part of this statement and reject the second. Some
believe the heavens were sprinkled with stars because of
numerous references to stars in the plays:

> yonder roof, that's nail'd so fast with stars

and

>   stars
> Stuck in yond' azure roof;

and

> the great star chamber o'er our heads

and

a million of glorious lights
That deck the heavenly canopy.

They have even cited the following passage from *Titus
Andronicus,* Act IV, scene 3, to support their contention that
"the heavens" were painted with the signs of the zodiac as
well as with stars: (Titus and his kinsman are shooting
messages to the gods fastened to arrows which they aim
straight up into the sky.)

TITUS.   Now, masters, draw. O well said, Lucius!
         Good boy, in Virgo's lap! Give it to Pallas.
MARC.   My lord, I aim a mile beyond the moon;
         Your letter is with Jupiter by this.
TITUS.   Ha, ha!
         Publius, Publius, what hast thou done?
         See, see, thou hast shot off one of Taurus' horns!
MARC.   This was the sport, my lord, when Publius shot,
         The bull, being gall'd, gave Aries such a knock
         That down fell both the Ram's horns in the court.

Surely there can be no feebler proof of the decoration of
the stage cover than quotations from actors who are pretending
to be out of doors. One might as well point to Lorenzo's famous
line, Act V, scene 1, in *The Merchant of Venice,* "How sweet
the moonlight sleeps upon this bank" as evidence that Shakespeare's comedies were produced only at full moon! Scholars
are enthusiasts and, as some Elizabethan might have said,
"Enthusiasm breeds strange argument."

The best reasons for believing the heavens were decorated
are that Malone says so and that the theaters of the Restoration
are known to have had some such paintings on the stage covers.

At least one, possibly two trap doors were cut in the heavens,
perhaps hinged, but more likely covered with canvas in which
a slit allowed the passage of an angel or fairy or divine being
down to the stage below by means of a flying machine. Like
the trap door into "hell," the trap leading to "heaven" was
inherited from the morality plays, or perhaps goes even
further back to the *deus ex machina* of the Greek theater. The
flying mechanism, the attendants to work it, and the actor

to be flown were all housed in what was called the "hut." The machine was a system of winding drums, counterweights, and escapements either for a flying throne, carriage, or chariot, or for a free flight.

In Posthumus's dream, in *Cymbeline,* Act V, scene 4, Jupiter descends, to the accompaniment of thunder and lightning, upon an eagle. This is the first use of an eagle in place of the throne or chariot formerly employed. An early seventeenth-century Italian theater print shows a similar flight: Jupiter descends astride a gigantic eagle that appears to have a wingspread of nearly ten feet. There are four wires or chains attached to the bird's body to keep it from swaying during its downward flight.

The flying machine was probably used for the witches in *Macbeth* also. Like all supernatural beings connected with the lower regions, the witches emerged from the trap door, probably in a cloud of smoke or vapor produced in the cellar by "fulminating powder." When they vanished, at the end of Act I, scene 1, the following lines suggest that they flew off:

> Fair is foul, and foul is fair;
> Hover through the fog and filthy air.

They may in Shakespeare's time, however, have vanished in the mist, although during the Restoration they are known to have flown. *Macbeth* was one of the most popular of Shakespeare's plays, never absent from the stage for long; Pepys saw it a number of times. There is no reason for supposing it was always staged in the same way. A verse appearing in *The Gentleman's Magazine* for October, 1760, suggests, in fact, that the productions varied:

> Say, ladies, have you never seen
> Spectators of the magic scene?
> Whether the fate of great Macbeth
> Or Harlequin's love, birth, or death,
> When after many a thunder clap,
> Grim witches vanish through a trap;
> Or haply the confed'rate hags

> Use broomsticks for aerial nags;
> But whether they may sink or soar,
> The beldames are beheld no more.

On the English stage the flying throne or car dates as far
back as 1587, although the free flight is supposed not to have
been introduced until 1611 when Ariel flew down from "the
heavens" in a production of *The Tempest* in Whitehall Palace.
In Italy free-flying goes back much further. Isabella d'Este,
writing to her husband in 1503, described a pageant of the
Annunciation which she had seen at the house of an archbishop: "The sky opened, revealing the figure of God the
Father, surrounded by a choir of angels. No support could
be seen either for His feet or for those of the angels, and six
other seraphs hovered in the air, suspended by chains. . . .
Then, all of a sudden, an infinite number of lights broke out
at the foot of the angel choir, and hid them in a blaze of
glory. . . . At that moment the Angel Gabriel alighted on the
ground, and the iron chain which he held was not seen, so
that he seemed to float down on a cloud." The clouds were
made of cotton batting; the angels were held by iron girdles
and were kept upright by weights of lead. A hundred years
later Ariel flew by similar means. Both Henry VII and
Henry VIII imported Italian artists, craftsmen, and workmen,
and it is possible that some of them brought designs for
flying machines with them.

The machine was put to less spectacular use in *Antony and
Cleopatra,* Act IV, scene 15. Cleopatra and her maids are aloft
in the monument; the dying Antony is brought in below, by
the guard. She is unable to descend to him, nor does she dare
to let her gate be opened, yet for a death scene it is important
for the mourner to be near the mourned. The lines of the
play make the action implicit:

CLEOPATRA.   How now? Is he dead?
DIOMEDES.   His death's upon him, but not dead.
              Look out o' th' other side your monument;
              His guard have brought him hither.
CLEOPATRA.   O sun,
              Burn the great sphere thou mov'st in! Darkling stand

> The varying shore o' th' world. O Antony,
> Antony, Antony! Help, Charmian; help, Iras; help!
> Help, friends below! let's draw him hither.

Cleopatra is obviously on the upper level of the inner stage, or in one of the window stages, probably the former, since she goes to the other side to look out of the monument, an action that would be easier to perform on a balcony than in a bay window. Antony, probably lying on his shield, is hoisted up by a rope apparently let down by Cleopatra and her women. The rope is actually attached to the windlass of the flying machine and Antony is slowly raised to Cleopatra's level, slowly not only to add to the solemnity and suspense, but to reduce the creaking of the machinery so that it will not interfere with the twenty-five lines that are spoken between Cleopatra's "Help, friends below! let's draw him hither," and her "Welcome, welcome" when he is near enough for her last kisses.

The inevitable creaking that accompanied the raising of the trap or the winding of the flying machine was covered up usually by the rumble of thunder, produced by the stagehands in the huts. Thunder was made by rolling a "bullit" (cannon ball) or a round stone across the floor of the heavens. *Othello* refers to this practice in Act V, scene 2: "Are there no stones in heaven But what serves for thunder?"

The production of lightning was described in detail by an Italian named Serlio, whose book, although not translated into English until 1611, was known before then. Sulphur or "vernis" powder was put into a box with a perforated cover. A stagehand, mounted on a ladder, shook the box into a lighted candle and the resulting flash made an extremely good imitation of sheet lightning. Forked lightning was prepared in a more elaborate fashion. A piece of wire covered with "pure gold" or "shining satten" was let down from above with a squib at the end, which was set on fire by what seems to have been a very difficult and tricky maneuver: "While the Bullit is rolling you must shoote off some piece of Ordinance, and with the same giving fire to the squibs."

Suns and moons, blazing comets, and similar meteoric displays were let down on to the stage by black threads attached to rings at the back. In addition to managing all these properties, the stagehands above the stage fired cannons and made appropriate noises for battles, bombardments, and salutes.

One might suppose, judging by the elaborate machinery described above, that the Shakespearean stage employed a great deal of scenery, but such is not the case. Scenery of the most lavish kind was used in masques, in "spectacles," and sometimes in connection with plays presented at court, but not, apparently, in the public theaters. There are accounts of scenery being used in public spectacles long before Shakespeare's time, as, for example, the following description of Henry VII's entry into London accompanied by Emperor Charles in 1521:

> They came to a Stockes where there was a quadrant stage where on was an Herber [arbor] full of Roses, Lyllies, and all other flowers curiously wrought, and byrds, beastes, and all other thynges of pleasure. And about the Herber was made the water full of Fyshe, and about it was the Elementes, the Planettes and Starres in their places *and everything moved,* and in a Type in the Toppe was made the Trinitie with the Angels singing, and the Trinitie blessed the Kyng and the Emperor, and under his feet was written, *behold the lover of peace and concorde.* [Later] they came to the little Conduite in Chepe where was buylded a place like heaven curiously painted with clouds, erbes [orbs], starres and the hierarchies of angels; in the top of this pageant was a great type and out of this type sodainly issued out of a cloud a fayre Lady richely appareled, and then al the minstrels which wer in the pageant plaied and the angels sang. And sodainly againe she was assumpted into the cloude which was very curiously done.

One of the most interesting of all Shakespearean studies is a book by Leslie Hotson entitled *The First Night of Twelfth Night* (1954), an account of the "revels" for Queen Elizabeth on January 6, 1600/1. The book reads like a detective story, as well it might, for its author is a kind of literary Sherlock Holmes who some years ago discovered the murderer of Christopher Marlowe. By studying old records Hotson came to the conclusion that *Twelfth Night* was written for the specific occasion, Ben Jonson's *Cynthia's Revels* having been found unsuitable. Apparently the Lord Chamberlain's Men had only eleven days to prepare for the production and rehearse the play, which was given in the Great Hall of Whitehall Palace on a small stage built for the purpose. The author believes, and argues most persuasively, that the production was "in the round." The record states: "In the Hall, which was richly hanged and degrees [tiers of seats] placed rownd about it." The phrase "rownd about it" means not "here and there" but "in a ring around it," according to Hotson's theory.

The stage was placed not far from Elizabeth's throne, with spectators on all four sides. The problem of the actors' entrances and exits was ingeniously solved by the use of "mansions"; that is, little houses made of wooden frames covered with canvas painted in perspective to suggest palaces or pavilions. The mansions had doors, or curtains at the doorways, behind which the actors could await their entrance cues and behind which they could retire, thereby averting the awkwardness of having to walk out through the audience. When the play was over, the stage, which was put together with wooden pins or pegs, could be taken apart and the mansions could be folded up like tents, to be stored until the players came to Whitehall again.

Dr. Hotson has made an extremely convincing case for the theater-in-the-round; he even believes that the Globe theater used mansions instead of the inner stage and that the audience completely surrounded the acting area, but his colleagues have not accepted his reconstruction of the Globe.

In the summer of 1605 a dramatic representation was produced in Oxford, for the king, for which Inigo Jones designed the scenery. A contemporary description runs as follows:

The stage was built close to the upper end of the hall, as it seemed at first sight. But indeed it was but a false wall fair painted and adorned with stately pillars, which pillars would turn about; by reason thereof, with the help of other painted cloths, their stage did vary three times in the acting of one Tragedy.

In spite of all the accounts of elaborate scenery at court, most scholars agree that, in the public theater as Shakespeare knew it, it did not exist. They base this opinion on two grounds.

The first is the absence of any references to scenery in contemporary accounts of the public theaters; the second is the absence of any records of money spent for scenery. Records for some of the playhouses have survived and there are some very curious items in the list of properties used at the Rose:

  1 rock, 1 cage, 1 tomb, 1 Hell mouth
  2 steeples and 1 chime of bells, and 1 beacon
  1 globe and 1 golden sceptre, 3 clubs
  1 golden fleece, 2 rockets, 1 bay tree
  1 lion skin, 1 bear skin
  Cupid's bow and quiver, the cloth of the sun and moon
  2 fanes of feathers, 1 tree of golden apples
  1 chain of dragons, 1 gilt spear
  1 lion, 1 great horse with his legs
  1 Pope's mitre
  1 black dog
  1 cauldron for the Jew

but, with the possible exception of "the cloth of the sun and moon," all these strange things must be considered properties rather than scenery.

Although most critics agree that little if any scenery was used, they are divided on the question of placards or signboards. Some years ago it was generally believed that signboards were put up on the stage to tell where the action took place, a belief that was based on contemporary reference to such a device. Sir Philip Sidney alludes to "Thebes written in great letters on an old doore," in 1583; and a quotation at the beginning of William Percy's *The Faery Pastorall,* or *Forrest of Elves,* produced by the Children of Paul's in about 1600, states: "Highest aloft and on the top of the Musick Tree, the Title, *The Faery Pastorall.* Beneath him pind on Post of the Tree the Scene *Eluida Forrest."* But today many scholars are not so sure that this practice was followed. In most of Shakespeare's plays, they point out, the opening lines of a scene tell the audience where it takes place. There are, of course, exceptions; in scene 1, Act III, of *All's Well That Ends Well,* the Duke of Florence enters with two French lords and a troop of soldiers, but there is nothing in the text to reveal who he is or where the action takes place. The pro-placard forces pounce upon this scene as evidence that sign-boards must have been used.

These are, however, very minor disagreements. In general, most stage historians agree that little, if any, scenery was in general use in the public theaters, and that this lack of setting was responsible, as one points out, for some of Shakespeare's most beautiful poetry. The picture conjured up in the imagination by such lines as these from *A Midsummer Night's Dream,* Act II, scene 2:

> I know a bank whereon the wild thyme blows,
> Where oxlips and the nodding violet grows,
> Quite over-canopied with luscious woodbine,
> With sweet musk-roses, and with eglantine:
> There sleeps Titania sometime of the night,
> Lull'd in these flowers with dances and delight;
> And there the snake throws her enamell'd skin,
> Weed wide enough to wrap a fairy in:

is richer than all the "fair painted cloths" of the Italian stage.

The outer stage is believed to have been painted, if only to protect it from the weather, and it was strewn with rushes, a usual procedure in Elizabethan times, to which Shakespeare makes a number of references. In *Romeo and Juliet,* Act I, scene 4, Romeo exclaims:

> A torch for me! Let wantons light of heart
> Tickle the senseless rushes with their heels . . .
> I'll be a candle-holder and look on,

revealing that even on a dance floor rushes were used. In *Cymbeline,* Act II, scene 2, Jachimo says:

> Our Tarquin thus
> Did softly press the rushes ere he waken'd
> The chastity he wounded.

In *The Taming of the Shrew,* Act IV, scene 1, there is another reference in Grumio's speech:

> Is supper ready, the house trimm'd, rushes strew'd,
> cobwebs swept . . . ?

as well as in *Henry IV,* Part I, Act III, scene 1, in which Glendower says to Hotspur:

> She bids you on the wanton rushes lay you down
> And rest your gentle head upon her lap.

The rushes would have served to protect the elaborate costumes from dust and dirt when the actors sat, or fell, or died on the floor of the stage. It has also been suggested that the rushes were used to suggest turf. When Richard II says, in Act III, scene 3,

> While here we march
> Upon the grassy carpet of the plain

and Iris, in *The Tempest,* Act IV, scene 1,

> The queen o' th' sky
> Whose wat'ry arch and messenger am I,
> Bids thee leave these, and with her sovereign grace,
> Here on this grass-plot, in this very place

it is true that the rushes would add verisimilitude, but it is much more likely that rushes were strewn on the floor because it was the custom to do so.

An indoor scene was represented very simply by hanging curtains along the back of the inner stage. To a modern audience the curtains might look odd, but, to a people accustomed for centuries to hanging tapestries or curtains on cold damp walls to reduce the chill and cut down on icy drafts, curtains appeared the proper hangings for a room. A few pieces of furniture could be carried in while the stage curtains were closed during a scene acted on another part of the stage. A bed signified a "chamber," a *prie-dieu* a chapel, a desk a "closet," for Queen Gertrude's "closet," in spite of Sir Laurence Olivier's film of *Hamlet,* was not a bedroom at all, but a small writing room or study.

It is possible that painted cloths were used to some extent, a woodland cloth to suggest an outdoor setting, a stone or brickwork cloth for battlements and base-court scenes. The free-standing doorposts and the posts of the outer stage could double as tree trunks, and served as convenient hiding places when actors were supposed to conceal themselves. It was probably behind a doorpost that Roderigo hid, following Iago's directions in *Othello,* Act V, scene 1:

> Here, stand behind this bulk: straight will he come.
> Wear thy good rapier bare, and put it home.

It was possibly also used in *Romeo and Juliet,* Act V, scene 3, when Paris, warned by his page of Romeo's approach, conceals himself.

Except for a few dissenting voices, stage historians agree that little scenery was used in Shakespeare's plays. How then is one to account for the contemporary references to the magnificent settings, a point that the dissenters are constantly bringing up? In 1600 Dudley Carleton wrote home that a play he saw in Amsterdam "might not be compared to your plays at London for stately setting forth in stage and apparel." Another traveler writes that the Venetian theater seemed "very beggarly and bare in comparison of our stately playhouses in England," and a third says, "For variety and magnificence of plays, England in our modern age surpassed all nations." The reader does not have to be very observant to notice that only the first of these three comments has any bearing on the *setting* of the plays. That the English *plays* were varied and magnificent no one could deny; and the playhouses with their curtains of beautiful fabrics and glowing colors and their delicate balustrades and carved posts must have been stately indeed. Only Dudley Carleton's verdict remains to be dealt with. Perhaps the explanation of his phrase "stately setting forth in stage" is to be found not in the scenery, but in the properties of the playhouse: "1 golden fleece, 2 rockets, 1 bay tree; 2 fanes of feathers, 1 tree of golden apples; 1 chain of dragons, 1 gilt spear"—surely such glittering objects would contribute a great deal to the "stately setting forth in stage." Combined with the magnificence of Shakespearean stage costumes, the effect must have been dazzling; and everyone is agreed that the costumes were rich and sumptuous. A Renaissance courtier always had his hat and his cloak or cape with him, even indoors, a fashion that was aped by all who wished to appear well dressed, and the stage must have been a blaze of silken banners, nodding plumes, and rich fabrics in many a scene: even without any painted cloths the productions must have been exceedingly impressive.

The scenery, then, was suggestive rather than realistic, but some of the properties were not only realistic but *real*. When Birnam Wood came to Dunsinane in Act V, scene 5 of *Macbeth,* the actors carried real branches of trees. Yorick's skull as well as the other skulls and bones thrown out by the gravedigger in scene 1, Act V of *Hamlet* were the genuine article; why waste time making imitation skulls when real ones were turned up in ploughed fields or excavations rather frequently in those days? It is interesting to see how long this somewhat grisly practice survived. In 1755 a critic objected to the use of "real Skulls and Bones," and a century later a reviewer in *The Theatrical Journal* protested that the use of human skulls and bones was "highly indecent, and at the same time repulsive to the audience." Even in America the practice was so common that a stagehand, a gas-lighter at the famous old Walnut Street theater in Philadelphia, bequeathed his own skull "to be used in the graveyard scene of *Hamlet"* after his death.

Sir Frank Benson, a Shakespearean actor of the late nineteenth century, always made his first appearance, in the part of Caliban, with a real fish in his mouth; he believed that in so doing he was following the practice established in Shakespeare's time, and there is at least a possibility that he was right. Actors are inclined to be great traditionalists, and as Shakespearean plays have been produced, sometimes in strangely modified form, to be sure, ever since the Restoration of the theaters, there has always been someone to pass the traditions down. Thomas Betterton, who played Shakespearean rôles when the theaters reopened and whose acting was so much admired by Samuel Pepys, was instructed by two old actors who had played with Shakespeare himself and who presumably followed his instructions.

If little is known for certain about the acting, a good deal is known about the actors. In Shakespeare's day there were twenty different adult companies playing in London alone, and more in the provinces. The names of more than five hundred actors are known today, and much more than mere names is known about some of them. Official records sometimes reveal strange sidelights, such as that Shakespeare was one of nine actors who marched in a procession celebrating James I's entrance into London on March 15, 1604, and was given four and a half yards of scarlet cloth for a cloak for the occasion.

There were no women in any actors' companies before the Restoration; all Shakespeare's lovely heroines were portrayed by boys:

HAMLET. Do the boys carry it away?
ROSENCRANTZ. Ay, that they do, my lord; Hercules and his load too.

If anyone doubts the truth of Rosencrantz's reply, Act II, scene 2, he need only attend a well-directed and seriously produced Shakespearean play at one of the better private schools for boys in order to be convinced. Then let him remember that the children of Shakespeare's time were not only excellently trained in singing, dancing, reciting, and acting, but that their livelihood depended on the success of their performance.

Ben Jonson gives us information about the age of the boy actors in his *Epitaph on Salathiel Pavy, a Child of Queen Elizabeth's Chapel,* in which he writes:

> Years he number'd scarce thirteen
> When Fates turn'd cruel,
> Yet three fill'd zodiacs had he been
> The stage's jewel.

Bearing in mind the fact that one of the children played the part of Cleopatra, one realizes the double-edged wit and irony in her lines in Act V, scene 2:

> . . . I shall see
> Some squeaking Cleopatra boy my greatness
> I' the posture of a whore.

It adds to the fun, too, of scene 2, Act I of *A Midsummer Night's Dream,* when Peter Quince is selecting his cast for his play:

QUINCE.   Flute, you must take Thisby on you.
FLUTE.   What is Thisby? a wand'ring knight?
QUINCE.   It is the lady that Pyramus must love.
FLUTE.   Nay, faith, let me not play a woman. I have a beard coming.
QUINCE.   That's all one. You shall play it in a mask, and you may speak as small as you will.

Peter Quince's amateur company brings up another subject in the same scene that was a cause of concern to actors: the danger of being arrested for offending some important person.

BOTTOM.   Let me play the lion too. I will roar that I will do any man's heart good to hear me; I will roar that I will make the Duke say, "Let him roar again; let him roar again."
QUINCE.   An you should do it too terribly, you would fright the Duchess and the ladies, that they would shriek; and that were enough to hang us all.
ALL.   That would hang us, every mother's son.

The Children of the Revels of Blackfriars endangered their freedom in acting *Eastward Hoe,* about 1604. Passages ridiculing the Scots, and even making fun of the dialect of the king, offended the court; fortunately for the children, the royal wrath was deflected to the three authors, Marston, Chapman, and Jonson, who were put in prison, where they might have remained for some time except for the intercession of friends in power.

No account of the theater in Shakespeare's day would be complete without a note on the audiences. When the players performed at court or in the great houses in the country, as they often did in the summer when the London theaters were closed because of the plague, Shakespeare may have had just the sort of listeners he most enjoyed. Here were lords and ladies, educated in the highest tradition of the Renaissance, who delighted in fine poetry. The elaborate figures in Romeo's first speeches in *Romeo and Juliet,* Act I, scene 1:

> Love is a smoke rais'd with the fume of sighs;
> Being purg'd, a fire sparkling in lovers' eyes;
> Being vex'd, a sea nourish'd with lovers' tears:
> What is it else? a madness most discreet,
> A choking gall, and a preserving sweet.

must have struck a responsive chord in the breasts of gallants who composed for their mistresses sonnets made of just such Petrarchan metaphors as these. Courtiers who frequently played at rhymed riddles would have been delighted with the song in *The Merchant of Venice,* Act III, scene 2:

> Tell me where is fancy bred,
> Or in the heart or in the head?
> How begot, how nourishèd?

and would have guessed, even before Bassanio did, that the casket containing Portia's portrait was the one made of lead, because of the rhyming clue.

Whether Shakespeare enjoyed the rabble in the pit is not so certain. In *Hamlet,* Act III, scene 2, the Prince of Denmark speaks disparagingly of the "groundlings, who for the most part are capable of nothing but inexplicable dumbshows and noise," and some critics have interpreted this to mean that the poet despised them. It may, on the other hand, have been a good-natured joke, not intended to imply any disapproval at all. A much more reliable source of information is found in letters, diaries, and public statements and writings of the time. Here we find Shakespeare's audiences fare very badly. Henry Crosse, writing of the typical theatergoers in 1603, says: "Now the common haunters are for the most part the lewdest persons in the land, apt for pilfery, perjury, forgery, or any rogueries, the very scum, rascality, and baggage of the people, thieves, cut-purses, shifters, cozeners; briefly, an unclean generation and spawn of vipers: must not here be good rule, where is such a brood of Hell-bred creatures? for a Play is like a sink in a town, whereunto all the filth doth run . . ."

Crosse's highly unfavorable verdict was accepted by E. K. Chambers, who agreed that the theater brought bad characters together, where they picked pockets, incited riots, started fights, and carried on "intrigues and other nefarious transactions." He mentions as further evidence Lady Bacon's anxious warning to her son to choose a more respectably located lodginghouse than one near the theaters. Aside from the fact that anxious mothers are the last people to be objective witnesses, there is a vagueness about the charges that Chambers makes. What intrigues? What nefarious transactions? One longs to know.

The paradox of the lowest persons in the land flocking to listen to the loftiest poetry is one that captures the imagination. Alfred Harbage, a Shakespearean historian, became so much interested in the subject that after years of sifting hundreds of documents—theater records, vital statistics, statutes, letters, and diaries among others—he established a very convincing case in favor of Shakespeare's much maligned audience.

To understand the attacks on the London playgoers it is necessary to look again at the enemies of the theater. The first group, the Puritans, who considered all pleasure a net spread by the devil to snare the ungodly, would naturally dislike the patrons of the theater. The city fathers may have been influenced by Puritan disapproval, but their primary objections to the theater were practical ones. They were afraid that people crowding together would spread the plague, a danger that was never long absent from London, and at the first indications of an epidemic the theaters were closed. They were also afraid of riots, and with some reason. English mobs were excitable and the city had no adequate means of dealing with them. At the theater two traditional enemies, the apprentices and the young men "in service" to some nobleman, were likely to meet, often with violent results. One such encounter at the Swan theater ended in a fatal stabbing. The apprentices had earned a bad name for themselves by their destructive behavior on Shrove Tuesday, when it was the tradition to demolish the brothels of Bankside, possibly with the virtuous intention of removing a temptation before the beginning of Lent in a manner not only easier than abstention, but better sport.

On at least one occasion, the destruction spread to the

theaters; a letter written in 1606 by John Chamberlain to Sir
Dudley Carleton describes the rioting: "On the 4th of this
month, being our Shrove Tuesday, the 'prentices, or rather
the unruly people of the suburbs, played their parts in divers
places, as Finsburg Fields about Wapping, by St. Catherine's,
and in Lincoln's Inn Fields, in which places, being assembled
in great numbers, they fell to great disorders, in pulling
down of houses, and beating of guards that were set to
keep rule, especially at a new playhouse, some time a cockpit,
in Drury Lane where the Queen's players used to play. Though
the fellows defended themselves as well as they could and
slew three of them with shot, and hurt divers, yet they
entered the house and defaced it, cutting the players' apparel
into pieces, and all their furniture, and burst their playbooks,
and did what mischief they could."

To the skeptical reader wondering why the apprentices,
who, although without any money except what they could
beg from their parents or masters, flocked in droves to the
theater, should destroy the playhouse and the costumes and
properties of the actors, Harbage points out that it is the
football fans who tear down the goal posts. Possibly a better
explanation could be found in a further examination of the
passage. The writer says " 'prentices, *or rather the unruly
people of the suburbs.*" Perhaps the apprentices have been
blamed for violence they had no hand in at all.

The third and most valid reason for the City Council's
enmity to the theaters lies in the ever-present danger of fire.
Although the plays were given in the afternoon and artificial
lights were not used in the public theaters, there seems to
have been a great deal of firing of cannons, lighting of squibs,
and setting on fire of rocks drenched in spirits. It is a wonder
more theaters did not end as the first Globe ended, burned
to the ground. Several accounts of the fire of June 29, 1613,
are in existence; according to Stowe's *Annals:* "Upon St.
Peter's day last, the playhouse or theatre called the Globe,
upon the Bankside, near London, by negligent discharge of
a peal of ordnance, close to the south side thereof, the thatch
took fire, and the wind suddenly dispersed the flames round

about, and in a very short space the whole building was quite consumed; and no man hurt: the house being filled with people to behold the play, viz. of Henry the Eight."

Sir Henry Wotton wrote in somewhat more detail of the event. "Now King Henry, making a masque at the Cardinal Wolsey's house, and certain cannons being shot off at his entry, some of the paper or other stuff wherewith one of them was stopped, did light on the thatch, where being thought at first but an idle smoke, and their eyes more attentive to the show, it kindled inwardly, and ran round like a train, consuming within less than an hour the whole house to the very ground. This was the fatal period of that virtuous fabrick; wherein yet nothing did perish but wood and straw, and a few forsaken cloaks." The fire confined itself to the Globe, although it might very well have spread. The Great Fire of 1666 that swept over four hundred acres, destroying St. Paul's, eighty-seven churches, and over thirteen thousand houses started with a small blaze in a baker's house. One can sympathize strongly with the dislike of the theater, a dislike that included the theatergoers as well.

A third group was mentioned earlier as being hostile to the playhouses and especially to the audiences, a group much larger than the other two and including many of their members, which might be called the antidemocratic faction. Today it is hard to understand the attitude, almost universally held for centuries, that the laboring man was put into the world for the sole purpose of working for his betters. The Emersonian distinction between the "working man" and "man working" would have been incomprehensible to the citizen of the Renaissance. The function of a laborer was to labor, and the sight of the working classes enjoying themselves at the theater was something contrary to the laws of God and nature, a perversion, in fact, and therefore shocking. In spite of the fact that Thomas Dekker wrote "Honest labour bears a lovely face," he had no desire to have that face close to his own. In 1609 he protested that the theater "is so free in entertainment, allowing a stoole as well to the Farmers sonne as to your Templer, that your Stinckard has the selfe-same libertie to be there . . . which your sweet courtier hath; and that your car-man and Tinker claime as strong a voice in their suffrage, and sit to give judgement on the plaies life and death as well as the prowdest Momus among the tribe of Critick."

Several passages in Shakespeare's plays have led some critics to believe that he too hated the masses, such as Casca's speech in *Julius Caesar,* Act I, scene 2, describing the citizen of Rome offering the crown to Caesar: "The rabblement shouted and clapped their chopped hands, and threw up their sweaty nightcaps, and uttered such a deal of stinking breath because Caesar refused the crown, that it almost choked Caesar," and *Coriolanus,* Act III, scene 3, in which Coriolanus rages against the citizens as follows:

> You common cry of curs! whose breath I hate
> As reek o' the rotten fens, whose loves I prize
> As the dead carcases of unburied men
> That do corrupt my air . . .

It is always well to bear in mind that an author is not to be judged by speeches he puts into the mouths of his characters, but if Shakespeare disliked the masses, he was merely sharing an almost universal prejudice.

Since the testimonials of such a large number of writers are found to be tainted by disapproval stemming from three possible sources, the most reliable evidence about Shakespeare's audience is to be found in private letters and diaries, and in the reports of foreign travelers. Sober, respectable citizens have revealed in their correspondence that they attended a play at the Globe, taking with them their wives or sisters, and nothing is said about the dangers of assault, insults, or inconvenience resulting from such ventures. As for the reports of travelers, Thomas Platter reported in 1597, "indeed men and womenfolk visit such places without scruple"; in 1602 Philip Julius wrote that "there are always a good many people present, including many respectable women"; and in 1614 Father Busino said "These theatres are frequented by a number of respectable and handsome ladies, who come freely and seat themselves among the men without the slightest hesitation."

Shakespeare's audiences, then, were made up of a cross section of the population—young men and their girls, married folk, noblemen, tradesmen, laborers, students, and apprentices. Harbage's study of statistics of the time led him to believe that the playgoers were for the most part young people. The theater was a favorite haunt of the students, of whom there were about eight hundred in London in 1595, and a thousand in the reign of James I. The apprentices outnumbered the students by ten to one and they too flocked to the theater whenever they could get a holiday, or steal one. Many of them must have been habitués, since Dekker says sourly "Every punk and her squire . . . can rand out by heart" the lines of the plays. They were a boisterous and noisy lot, quick to greet an unsuccessful performance with hisses, catcalls, and boos; quick to hail a successful one with cheers and shouts; unruly, perhaps, by modern standards, but not what an unprejudiced witness could call "an unclean generation and spawn of vipers."

The theater has undergone many changes since Shakespeare's lifetime; and although the staging may today be closer to that of the old Globe than the picture-frame staging of a hundred years ago, Shakespeare himself, could he be present at one of the new Globe theaters, would doubtless be far more impressed by the differences than by the similarities. But in one respect there has been no alteration—the audiences for Shakespearean plays are still young people. In schools and colleges, throughout the country students are rehearsing *Twelfth Night* or *Hamlet,* and at performances of professional companies the young outnumber the old. If, as pessimists claim, the young people of today are facing the cold gray dawn of an era of regimentation, they are still able to bask, at the Shakespearean theaters, in the golden light of the great age of the English Renaissance.

SUE G. WALCUTT

LIFE OF SHAKESPEARE

⚜ ⚜ ⚜

The facts as to the life of William Shakespeare are so meager that biographers have been hard put to it to decide where truth ends and legend begins. The first authentic date is the entry in the Parish Register, at Stratford-on-Avon, Warwickshire, England, which gives the date of baptism of *Gulielmus Filius Johannes Shakspere,* as April 26, 1564. Tradition assigns April 23 as the date of his birth.

John Shakespeare, the future dramatist's father, was a man of some means and local importance. He married, in 1557, Mary Arden, daughter of Robert Arden, a well-to-do farmer. To them eight children were born: the first three being Joan in 1558; Margaret in 1562; and William in 1564. Both of the girls died in infancy. The house in which William was born (at least it is one of two houses then owned by his father) is still preserved as a memorial.

About the age of seven, William Shakespeare began his attendance at the Free Grammar School at Stratford, but owing to financial reverses suffered by his father, he was withdrawn from school at fourteen, or thereabouts. Nothing, however, is definitely known concerning his occupation after leaving school. It is believed that he was apprenticed to a butcher.

The next definite date, and that of considerable importance, is 1582. In November of this year, when the young Shakespeare was only nineteen years of age, he was married to Anne Hathaway, twenty-seven. She was the daughter of a certain Richard Hathaway, a farmer in the neighboring village of Shottery. On May 26 of the following year their first child, Susanna, was baptized. In February, 1585, his twin children, Hamnet and Judith, were baptized.

From this time forward, Shakespeare's actions are difficult

to trace, other than in his stage work and authorship. Various strolling companies of actors visited Stratford between 1585 and 1590, and doubtless fanned into flame his latent desire to be an actor. According to a well-founded tradition, he became involved in a difficulty with Sir Thomas Lucy, a neighboring magistrate, over a deer-poaching adventure, and this hastened his departure for London. He at once sought employment at the theaters, and, it is said, first tended the horses outside the stage door; then was given minor parts; but soon demonstrated by his "admirable wit" his ability to take important leads. In 1592, when Shakespeare was twenty-eight, the first direct references to him as an actor and playwright appear. Robert Green issued a pamphlet entitled a "Groatsworth of Wit," in which he parodied a line from *Henry the Sixth,* Part III, and puns Shakespeare's name as "Shake-scene." Chettle, the publisher of his attack, in this same year, issued a public apology for it, in which he mentioned Shakespeare by name.

In the year 1593, *Venus and Adonis* appeared, and the dedication signed by William Shakespeare spoke of it as "the first heir of my invention." Then followed, in succeeding years, his dramas beginning with *Titus Andronicus.* In 1598, Francis Meres makes an important reference to Shakespeare the dramatist, enumerating a dozen of his plays, up to that time. We also find allusions to Shakespeare in connection with other well-known actors, Heming, Condell, Philips, Burbage, and others.

As an evidence of his growing prosperity, we find recorded under date of May 1, 1602, the purchase of 107 acres of arable land near Stratford, from William and John Coombe. Shakespeare acted before Queen Elizabeth, in 1603, and on the formal entry of King James into London, the following year, he was one of nine prominent actors who marched in the procession.

The next and closing ten years of his life were filled with affairs chiefly pertaining to the stage. A chronological list of his plays, as near as this can be ascertained, is given elsewhere in this volume. Other direct references to his activities are chiefly in the form of legal transfers of property, such as the purchase of a home in Stratford, called "New Place." The final reference is his will, signed in the year 1616, only a short time before his death which occurred April 23, probably on his fifty-second birthday.

His body was laid to rest in the church at Stratford, a flat stone with its now famous inscription being placed over the grave, and a bust being placed in the north wall of the chancel facing it. But by far the most famous monument to his memory is the First Folio Edition of his Plays, issued in 1623, seven years after his death, by his fellow actors. This definitely assigned the authorship of twenty hitherto unprinted plays, and included the others ascribed to Shakespeare during his lifetime, with the exception of *Pericles*. The First Folio is now the most highly treasured volume in the world, and when a copy occasionally finds its way from one collector's hands to another's, it fetches fabulous prices.

POEMS AND SONNETS

In addition to the thirty-seven plays credited to Shakespeare, his works include miscellaneous poems and sonnets as follows:

Venus and Adonis
The Passionate Pilgrim
The Rape of Lucrece
A Lover's Complaint
The Phoenix and Turtle
Sonnets.

VENUS AND ADONIS

This narrative poem first appeared in Quarto form, in 1593, without the author's name. The publisher was Richard Field. The popularity of the poem is attested by the issue of twelve different editions between 1593 and 1636. Although Shakespeare's name was not placed on the title-page, he signs a dedicatory page to the Earl of Southampton, in which he states that the poem is "the first heir of my invention." The poem consists of 199 verses of six lines each.

THE PASSIONATE PILGRIM

This series of sonnets and love poetry was first published in 1599, by W. Jaggard, and with Shakespeare's name on the title-page. In 1612, a second edition was published by Thomas Heywood. The book as a whole is doubtfully Shakespeare's. It consists of 21 sonnets and short pieces, some of which have been traced to other writers. It seems to have been issued by a piratical publisher in the endeavor to profit by Shakespeare's popularity.

THE RAPE OF LUCRECE

The first edition of *Lucrece* appeared as a Quarto, in 1594, without the author's name. It was "printed by Richard Field for John Harrison." Seven editions followed between 1594 and 1655. As in his earlier poem, Shakespeare signs a dedicatory page, in which he dedicates the poem to his friend and patron, the Earl of Southampton. The work is a long narrative poem of 265 verses, each with seven lines. It is based on a well-known story emanating from Latin writers, and also utilized by Chaucer in his "Legend of Good Women."

A LOVER'S COMPLAINT

This poem, which is written in the same meter as *The Rape of Lucrece,* evidently belongs to the same period. It was first published in 1609, at the end of the volume of *Sonnets.* It contains 47 verses.

THE PHOENIX AND TURTLE

A short poem of 13 four-line verses, followed by a "threnos" of five three-line verses, the whole thing being an allegory of doubtful meaning. It first appeared in a collection published in 1601, by Robert Chester.

SONNETS

One of the most interesting of all of Shakespeare's works is his collection of *Sonnets.* Irrespective of their high merit, they offer to critics a fertile field of investigation. They first appeared in 1609 with the title-page: "Shake-speare's Sonnets. Never before imprinted. At London, by G. Eld for T. T. and are to be sold by William Aspley, 1609." The sonnet sequence falls into three main divisions: (A) Sonnets 1-126; (B) Sonnets 127-152; and (C) Sonnets 153-154. The general theme is the poet's deep affection for a friend, a young man of exalted rank.

CHRONOLOGICAL ORDER OF
THE PLAYS

Much diversity of opinion exists as to the dates of composition of the plays. We append three lists on the authority of as many Shakespearean scholars. A dash placed in a column indicates disputed authorship:

	Malone	*Chalmers*	*Drake*
1. Titus Andronicus	——	——	——
2. King Henry the Sixth, Part I	1589	1593	——
3. King Henry the Sixth, Part II	1591	1595	1592
4. King Henry the Sixth, Part III	1591	1595	1592
5. The Two Gentlemen of Verona	1591	1595	1595
6. The Comedy of Errors	1592	1591	1591
7. King Richard the Second	1593	1596	1596
8. King Richard the Third	1593	1596	1595
9. Love's Labour's Lost	1594	1592	1591
10. The Merchant of Venice	1594	1597	1597
11. A Midsummer Night's Dream	1594	1598	1593
12. Romeo and Juliet	1596	1592	1593
13. King John	1596	1598	1598
14. The Taming of the Shrew	1596	1599	1594
15. King Henry the Fourth, Part I	1597	1597	1596
16. King Henry the Fourth, Part II	1599	1597	1596
17. King Henry the Fifth	1599	1597	1599
18. As You Like It	1599	1602	1600
19. Much Ado About Nothing	1600	1599	1599
20. Hamlet	1600	1598	1597
21. The Merry Wives of Windsor	1601	1596	1601
22. Troilus and Cressida	1602	1610	1601
23. Measure for Measure	1603	1604	1603
24. King Henry the Eighth	1603	1613	1602
25. Othello	1604	1614	1612
26. King Lear	1605	1605	1604

	Malone	Chalmers	Drake
27. All's Well That Ends Well	1606	1606	1598
28. Macbeth	1606	1606	1606
29. Julius Cæsar	1607	1607	1607
30. Twelfth Night	1607	1613	1613
31. Antony and Cleopatra	1608	1608	1608
32. Cymbeline	1609	1606	1605
33. Timon of Athens	1610	1611	1602
34. Coriolanus	1610	1619	1609
35. The Winter's Tale	1611	1601	1610
36. The Tempest	1611	1613	1611
37. Pericles	——	——	——

THE TEMPEST

❦ ❦ ❦

Present play contains 5 Acts, 9 Scenes, 2033 lines

CAST OF CHARACTERS

ALONSO, *King of Naples*
SEBASTIAN, *brother to Alonso*
PROSPERO, *the rightful Duke of Milan*
ANTONIO, *brother to Prospero, and usurping Duke of Milan*
FERDINAND, *son to the King of Naples*
GONZALO, *an honest old Counsellor*
ADRIAN, } *Lords*
FRANCISCO, }
CALIBAN, *a savage and deformed slave*
TRINCULO, *a jester*
STEPHANO, *a drunken butler*
Master of a ship
Boatswain
Mariners
MIRANDA, *daughter to Prospero*
ARIEL, *an airy Spirit*
IRIS,
CERES,
JUNO, } *Spirits*
NYMPHS,
REAPERS,
Other Spirits attending on Prospero
SCENE: *A ship at sea; an island*

ACT I

A tempest-tossed vessel is wrecked upon the shores of an
enchanted isle whereon dwell Prospero and his daughter,

51

Miranda, alone save for the presence of Caliban, a deformed and brutish slave. During the storm Prospero tells his daughter of his past life: Formerly he had been Duke of Milan, but had been supplanted by his brother Antonio, with the aid of Alonso, King of Naples, who desired thereby to render Milan tributary to his kingdom. The conspirators had not dared to kill Prospero outright, but had contented themselves with setting him and his daughter, then three years old, adrift in a crazy boat upon the open sea. They would have perished miserably but for a humane Neapolitan named Gonzalo, who provisioned their craft, and thus enabled them to reach the island which they made their home. For twelve years they had quietly dwelt there—a period spent profitably by Prospero in the education of his daughter and in his own study of works on magic. Prospero ends his story by telling Miranda that a strange chance has sent all of his enemies to him in the ship which they have seen wrecked in the tempest raised by his art. Ariel, the chief of his spirits, now appears and reports that all the passengers have been brought safely to land. Ferdinand, the King's son, becomes separated from the rest, and they suppose him lost. Prospero leads him to his cell, where the prince and Miranda become mutually enamoured.

ACT II

Alonso, Sebastian (his brother), Antonio, Gonzalo, and other victims of the shipwreck roam the island until all but Sebastian and Antonio are put to sleep by the invisible Ariel through the agency of gentle music. Sebastian and Antonio now plot to murder the King. Ariel frustrates their plans. In another part of the island two others of the company, Stephano and Trinculo, discover Caliban.

ACT III

The three last named plot to despatch Caliban's master, Prospero, and seize upon the island for themselves. The King and his company meanwhile wander about oppressed by weariness, hunger, and mental aberration. Ariel tantalises them with the vision of a spectral banquet. At his cell Prospero sets Ferdinand to the task of carrying and piling logs, in order, as later develops, to test the prince's affection for Miranda, who, on her part, entreats Ferdinand to let her share in his arduous labours.

ACT IV

Ferdinand undergoes the trial worthily, and Prospero bestows his daughter's hand upon him, and entertains the lovers with a glimpse into the land of spirits. The entertainment is interrupted by Prospero, who, suddenly recollecting the conspiracy of Caliban and his confederates, calls Ariel, and prepares to frustrate them. The conspirators meet with severe punishment at the hands of Prospero and Ariel, who set upon them "divers spirits in the shape of dogs and hounds."

ACT V

The King and his company are brought by Ariel before Prospero, who is moved to be merciful because of their sufferings. He reveals his identity to them. The King begs of him pardon for the wrongs he has done him, and restores to him his dukedom. Prospero brings forward Ferdinand and Miranda, whose troth is ratified by Alonso. Prospero abjures the mystic art, and with the King and his train proceeds to Naples, by means of the magically preserved ship, to solemnize the nuptials of the lovers.

NOTES

The first authenticated mention of *The Tempest* is found in the Rawlinson MSS. preserved in the Bodleian Library, which shows that the play was acted at Court, in 1613, during the festivities celebrating the wedding of a daughter of King James I. Other evidence indicates that it was written between the years 1610–1613, and first presented by John Heming's company of players.

FIRST EDITION. *The Tempest* was first printed in the First Folio Edition of Shakespeare's works, issued in 1623, a few years after the poet's death, by John Heming and Henry Condell, his friends and fellow actors. For some reason not now clear they gave this play precedence in the table of contents, although it is one of the latest ones in point of time of authorship.

SOURCES. As in other plays, Shakespeare drew his inspiration for *The Tempest* from other sources, partly historical, partly fictional. Several touches seem to be allusions to a shipwreck of Sir George Somers and his party in the Bermudas, as related in Jourdan's "Discovery of the Bermudas," published in 1610. The framework of the plot may have been derived from a story by the Spanish author Antonio de Eslava, found in his "Winter Nights," and published in Madrid, in 1609.

ACTION. The action of the play takes place during the afternoon of a single day, although references are made to happenings of twelve years preceding. The story hinges upon a plan by the banished duke, Prospero, to recover his lost fortunes. He had been defrauded of his dukedom of Milan by his brother, and cast away upon an island. He studies magic and invokes spirits good and bad to do his bidding; and the characters of the play are therefore about equally divided between the natural and the supernatural. The play itself is more nearly a fairy tale than any other proceeding from the dramatist's pen.

SELECTED CRITICISM. "Many commentators agree in the belief that *The Tempest* is the last creation of Shakespeare. I will readily believe it. There is in *The Tempest* the solemn tone of a testament. It might be said that, before his death, the poet, in this épopée of the ideal, has designed a codicil for the Future. In this enchanted isle, full of 'sounds and sweet airs that give delight' we may expect to behold Utopia, the promised land of future generations, Paradise regained. Who in reality is Prospero, the king of this isle? Prospero is the shipwrecked sailor who reaches port, the exile who regains his native land; he who from the depths of despair becomes all-powerful, the worker who by his science has tamed matter, Caliban, and by his genius the spirit, Ariel. Prospero is man, the master of Nature and the despot of destiny. He is the man—Providence!"— VICTOR HUGO.

THE TWO GENTLEMEN OF VERONA

❦ ❦ ❦

Present play contains 5 Acts, 20 Scenes, 2213 lines

CAST OF CHARACTERS

DUKE OF MILAN, *father to Silvia*
VALENTINE,
PROTEUS, } *the two Gentlemen of Verona*
ANTONIO, *father to Proteus*
THURIO, *a foolish rival to Valentine*
EGLAMOUR, *agent for Silvia in her escape*
HOST, *where Julia lodges*
OUTLAWS, *with Valentine*
SPEED, *a clownish servant to Valentine*
LAUNCE, *the like to Proteus*
PANTHINO, *servant to Antonio*
JULIA, *beloved of Proteus*
SILVIA, *beloved of Valentine*
LUCETTA, *waiting-woman to Julia*
Servants, Musicians

SCENE: *Verona; Milan; the frontiers of Mantua*

ACT I

Valentine and Proteus, two gentlemen of Verona, are intimate
friends accustomed to telling their hearts' secrets freely, the
one to the other. Valentine goes to the court of Milan to
gain worldly experience and honour. Proteus, for love of
a Veronese maiden named Julia, would fain stay at home;
but his father, ignorant of the love affair, and desirous that
his son shall see something of the world, sends him to join
Valentine at Milan.

ACT II

Silvia, the daughter of the Duke of Milan, has many suitors. No sooner does Valentine see her than he becomes one of the number; but he is more fortunate than the rest, for Silvia favours him. The Duke, however, has chosen another for his daughter's husband. Valentine and Silvia plan to elope. At this juncture Proteus arrives from Verona, after having exchanged vows there with Julia. Valentine introduces Proteus to Silvia, confides to him the secret of their proposed clandestine marriage, and asks his assistance. Proteus promises it, but inwardly resolves to play his friend false, and try to win Silvia for himself. His neglected love, Julia, hearing no tidings of him, decides to don boy's garments, and go to Milan in search of him.

ACT III

Proteus foils his friend's schemes by informing the Duke of the lovers' projected flight. The Duke banishes Valentine from his realm. Thurio, the suitor chosen by the Duke, does not prosper in his wooing; the two therefore ask Proteus, whom they know to be affianced, to lend his aid in furthering the match—which the false friend promises to do.

ACT IV

The banished Valentine flees to a forest near Milan, where he falls into the hands of outlaws, who, pleased by his address, make him their chief.

In Milan, Proteus plays false with Thurio just as he had done with Valentine. Under guise of fostering Thurio's suit he pleads his own cause to Silvia, who scorns him. Julia arrives dressed as a page, and secures employment with Proteus, who does not recognise her. She soon has opportunity to discover her lover's perfidy, since he sends her to Silvia with a ring that was Julia's own love-token to him.

ACT V

Silvia escapes to the forest in search of Valentine, but is seized by some of the outlaws of her lover's band. Before they can bring her to his presence, she is rescued by Proteus, who, however, tries to take advantage of the occasion and compel her to yield to his love. Valentine overhears his false friend and liberates Silvia, at the same time reproaching Proteus so sternly that the latter is stricken with remorse, and humbly begs forgiveness. The generous Valentine accords it. The identity of Julia is discovered, and she is united with her repentant lover.

Meantime the Duke, who had gone also to the forest in search of Silvia, is captured by others of Valentine's outlaws. Valentine releases him; and the Duke pardons all the band, permits them to resume the rights of citizenship, and consents to the nuptials of Silvia and Valentine.

NOTES

The only mention of *The Two Gentlemen of Verona* prior to its insertion in the First Folio Edition is found in the "Palladis Tamia" by Francis Meres (1598) where it is listed first among six comedies. It thus certainly antedates that year; and its general style has caused it to be placed among the dramatist's earliest productions, between 1591 and 1595.

FIRST EDITION. *The Two Gentlemen of Verona* was first printed in the First Folio of 1623. There is no mention of its having been performed in Shakespeare's lifetime; nor did it appear in any of the early Quartos. The listing by Meres above-mentioned, however, would seem to indicate that it was in active repertory during the first years of the dramatist's stage apprenticeship.

SOURCES. Certain coincidences in the plot suggest that it was derived in part from the "Diana" of Jorge de Montemayor, a Portuguese poet, which gives a similar story of a shepherdess, Filismena, who disguised as a page goes in quest of her forgetful lover. A theme along the same lines is found in a German play, "Julio and Hippolyta." Sir Philip Sidney's "Arcadia" is another romance which reflects incidents in "Diana"; and Shakespeare may have drawn his inspiration from Sidney rather than the Portuguese author. Indeed, romantic stories of this nature were plentiful and suggestions may have come to Shakespeare in a dozen different ways.

ACTION. The actual time supposed to elapse is seven days, but a much longer interval is indicated between scenes and acts. The first two scenes occur on the first day; then comes an interval of several weeks, during which Valentine goes from Verona to Milan. Similarly, there is a passing back and forth between cities of other characters, which in that day of slow travel necessarily consumed time. This, however, is only indicated, and the actual progress of the drama on the stage falls within seven days.

SELECTED CRITICISM. "Love, in its double form of sexual love and friendship, is evidently the basis of the whole, the leading centre of the action. To represent this foundation in its uncertainty and instability—in other words, to describe it within the comic view of life, in contradiction with its true nature, is manifestly the purport and tendency of the play. This is, however, too seriously and strongly emphasized, and thus the representation loses in comic power. Love is here, accordingly, represented in the most diversified forms, but invariably weak and frail, foolish and perverse."—ULRICI.

THE MERRY WIVES OF WINDSOR

❦ ❦ ❦

Present play contains 5 Acts, 23 Scenes, 2735 lines

CAST OF CHARACTERS

SIR JOHN FALSTAFF
FENTON, *a gentleman*
SHALLOW, *a country justice*
SLENDER, *cousin to Shallow*
FORD, } *two gentlemen dwelling at Windsor*
PAGE, }
WILLIAM PAGE, *a boy, son to Page*
SIR HUGH EVANS, *a Welsh parson*
DOCTOR CAIUS, *a French physician*
HOST *of the Garter Inn*
BARDOLPH, }
PISTOL, } *followers of Falstaff*
NYM, }
ROBIN, *page to Falstaff*
SIMPLE, *servant to Slender*
RUGBY, *servant to Doctor Caius*
MISTRESS FORD, *wife to Ford*
MISTRESS PAGE, *wife to Page*
ANNE PAGE, *daughter to Page*
MISTRESS QUICKLY, *servant to Doctor Caius*
Servants to Page, Ford, and others
SCENE: *Windsor, and its environs*

ACT I

Sir John Falstaff has forsaken the warlike pursuits familiar
to his friend Prince Hal, afterwards Henry V of England,
and is now devoted to the peaceful occupations of poaching

and love-making, though not neglecting the drinking-cups of the tavern. Two women of Windsor, Mistress Ford and Mistress Page, engage his attention at the same time; and he resolves to lay siege to their affections, notwithstanding both are married.

Mistress Page's daughter Anne is sought in marriage by Slender—largely through his friends; by Sir Hugh Evans, a Welsh curate and schoolmaster; by Doctor Caius, a French physician; and by Fenton, a courtier. The rivalry for the young woman's hand grows intense.

ACT II

Mistress Page and Mistress Ford each receive a love-letter from Falstaff, and upon comparing their missives they find them almost identical. Being women of wit as well as of virtue, they agree to work together towards humiliating the knight for his presumption. Mistress Ford makes an appointment with him. His servants inform the husbands of the two women. Ford, under an assumed name, meets Falstaff and, pretending to be a suitor also for Mistress Ford, worms from the boastful Falstaff the secret of his appointment with her.

ACT III

Falstaff is punctual to his meeting with Mistress Ford. But before he arrives, she and Mistress Page prepare a large basket of soiled linen in which Falstaff is to be conveyed to the river, under the pretense that this is the only way he can escape from the house. The pretense turns to reality when Ford actually arrives. And the ruse of the clothes-basket deceives both gallant and husband. Falstaff is dumped into the Thames, whence he emerges much bedraggled, but with ardour so slightly quenched as to become enkindled again upon receipt of a message from Mistress Ford granting him a second interview. Nor has he gained discretion from his first mishap, for he unwittingly informs Ford of this rendezvous also, and of the means whereby he escaped his former predicament. The thoroughly aroused husband redoubles his vigilance.

ACT IV

Falstaff keeps his second appointment with Mistress Ford. Her husband again surprises them. The clothes-basket is sent down as before; and while Ford is ransacking it under the firm belief that it again conceals Falstaff, the latter is dressed in woman's clothes and escapes thus disguised, though not avoiding sundry blows from the irate husband. Mistress Ford and Mistress Page then tell their husbands the truth about the Falstaff episodes. The men are delighted to find their wives faithful, and the four conjointly arrange a third and final hoax which contemplates a night meeting in Windsor Park.

Meanwhile Anne Page's love-affairs are becoming tangled. She loves Fenton. Her father has chosen Slender. Her mother privately favours Doctor Caius. When the third prank on Falstaff is prepared, Anne and her parents make conflicting plans to utilize the meeting for bringing their separate matrimonial schemes to a head.

ACT V

Falstaff is persuaded to go to Windsor Park, wearing a buck's head. Anne Page and her friends impersonate fairies and burn him with tapers. Ford, Page, and their wives reveal themselves to him, reproach him for his attempted villainy, and finally pardon him. The wretched Falstaff finds his only satisfaction in hearing that Anne Page has married Fenton, despite the counter-schemes of her father and mother.

NOTES

The Merry Wives of Windsor is said by several early writers to have been written and performed by special command of Queen Elizabeth, "who obliged Shakespeare to write a play of Sir John

Falstaff in love, and which I am very well assured he performed in a fortnight." Thus writes Gildon, in 1710; and Dennis, in 1702, mentions the same tradition. *Merry Wives* was probably written for the Christmas court revels of 1598 or 1599.

FIRST EDITIONS. A garbled text of the play probably taken from notes of a performance was published in Quarto form, in 1602; the title-page saying, "As it hath bene divers times acted by the right honorable my Lord Chamberlaines Servants. Both before her Majestie and elsewhere." A second Quarto appeared in 1619, which was a mere reprint of the first. In the authorized version of the First Folio, 1623, it is twice the length of the Quartos.

SOURCES. The story is evidently original with Shakespeare, although it contains situations common to other contemporary pieces. There are four or five other tales of the outwitting of jealous husbands, of that time, such as: "Il Pecerone," by Fiorentino; "Il Tredeci," by Strapola (both Italian); "Two Lovers of Pisa," by Tarlton; "The Unfortunate Lovers." These, however, suggest only the groundwork of a situation which Shakespeare develops and elaborates.

ACTION. The time of action on the stage is hard to follow clearly, but is either three or four days. It traces events in Falstaff's career, following his military and other exploits narrated in *Henry IV*. The epilogue to that historical play gives a promise to continue the story with Falstaff in it. The later play of *Henry V* merely narrates his death.

SELECTED CRITICISM. "Queen Bess can scarcely have been a great judge of art, or she would not have conceived the extravagant notion of wanting to see Falstaff in love; she would have understood that if there was anything impossible to him it was this. . . . The poet must have set himself unwillingly to the fulfilment of the wish, and tried to make the best of a bad business. He was compelled entirely to ruin his inimitable Falstaff, and degrade the fat knight into an ordinary avaricious, wine-bibbing, amatory old fool. Along with him he resuscitated the whole merry company from *Henry V*. . . . Bardolph, Pistol, Nym, and Dame Quickly."— BRANDES.

MEASURE FOR MEASURE

❧ ❧ ❧

Present play contains 5 Acts, 17 Scenes, 2704 lines

CAST OF CHARACTERS

VINCENTIO, *Duke of Vienna*
ANGELO, *Deputy to the Duke*
ESCALUS, *a venerable lord, and counsellor*
CLAUDIO, *a young gentleman*
LUCIO, *a fantastic*
Two other gentlemen
A Provost
THOMAS, ⎱ *friars*
PETER, ⎰
A Justice
VARRIUS
ELBOW, *a simple constable*
FROTH, *a foolish gentleman*
POMPEY, *servant to Mistress Overdone*
ABHORSON, *an executioner*
BARNARDINE, *a dissolute prisoner*
ISABELLA, *sister to Claudio*
MARIANA, *betrothed to Angelo*
JULIET, *beloved of Claudio*
FRANCISCA, *a nun*
MISTRESS OVERDONE, *a courtesan*
Lords, Gentlemen, Officers, Guards, Citizens, and Attendants
SCENE: *Vienna*

ACT I

Vincentio, Duke of Vienna, being desirous of introducing reforms into his government, particularly along the line of public morality, announces that he is to travel in distant lands, and delegates his authority to Angelo, a man renowned for probity in public and purity in private life. Instead of leaving the city, the Duke assumes the habit of a friar and remains to watch secretly the actions of his deputy.

Claudio, a young gentleman of Vienna, wrongs his betrothed, Juliet, who is with child by him. Though the lovers contemplate early marriage, Claudio becomes amenable to an old law—till then obsolete—which fixes capital punishment for his sin. And the stern Angelo, anxious to make a striking example of the first offender brought before him, sentences Claudio to death. The latter's sister, Isabella, is on the point of entering a nunnery, but being advised of her brother's peril, resolves to intercede with the deputy.

ACT II

Angelo vigorously prosecutes his work of reform in morality. In his zeal he has scant time for mercy; and Isabella at her first interview with him can obtain no leniency for her brother. But she awakens in Angelo a passion that had hitherto lain dormant in his cold nature. At her second interview with him he proposes in so many words that she purchase her brother's pardon with her own honour.

ACT III

The virtuous maiden spurns the proffered terms and hastens to Claudio, in prison, whom she exhorts to prepare for death, since his life can be procured only by her disgrace. Claudio at first upholds her decision; but the fear of death weakens his resolution, and he implores her to yield for his sake. Isabella, deeply angered, is on the point of leaving him to his fate, when the disguised Duke—who has heard their conversation—enters the cell. He tells Isabella privately of a way by which she can save her brother without compromising herself. It is by appearing to yield to Angelo, appointing a rendezvous with him, and then sending in her stead one

Mariana, who had been engaged in marriage to and then deserted by Angelo.

ACT IV

The Duke takes Isabella to Mariana's house, where the details of the plan are arranged. Angelo, having accomplished his purpose with the supposed Isabella, orders the immediate execution of Claudio. The Duke is in the prison when the order arrives, and finds means to save Claudio by displaying the head of another man who had just died and who resembled him. The Duke then advises his deputy by letter that he will shortly return to the city.

ACT V

The Duke appears at the city gates, clad in his proper costume. He is met by Angelo and other officials. Isabella publicly accuses Angelo of seduction and murder. The Duke feigns anger towards her and places her under arrest. Mariana in turn brings accusation. The Duke retires, leaving the inquiry in his deputy's hands, and shortly returns in his costume of friar in order to act as witness in the testimony of the two women. Circumstances in the trial force him to resume suddenly his rank as Duke; whereupon he visits merited condemnation upon Angelo, who is sentenced to death, after being married to Mariana for her own protection. The penalty is averted by the entreaties of the wife, seconded by the gentle Isabella. Claudio is released from prison and enjoined to wed with Juliet, while the Duke sues for the hand of Isabella.

NOTES

There is no reference to *Measure for Measure* anterior to its inclusion in the First Folio, except an entry in the "Court Revels" from October, 1604, to October, 1605, where it was said to have been played by "his Majesty's Players." This entry, however, is now believed to be spurious, although it may allude to an earlier actual record, as the play seems to belong to this period.

FIRST EDITION. The First Folio edition of 1623 contains the earliest known text of *Measure for Measure*. It is placed fourth in order of printing among the comedies.

SOURCES. This play was derived from two earlier sources, but shows an advance upon both. The first of these is an Italian tale found in Cinthio's "Hecatommithi," a collection similar to Boccaccio's "Decameron." But the more direct source was probably a play by George Whetstone, "Promos and Cassandra," written about 1578 but not produced on the stage.

ACTION. The duration of action is four days, after allowing for the introductory first scene. The period according to Whetstone's story is the time of Corvinus, King of Hungary, who died in 1490—or the close of the fifteenth century. But the plot has little to do with any particular country or time. It is an interplay of intrigue, jealousy, and wrong which is only saved from tragedy by a gleam of justice at the close.

SELECTED CRITICISM. "The city of Vienna is the scene of the play— it is represented as a very sink of sensual defilement, corrupted and ravaged in every physical and moral quality. . . . The progress of public demoralization is rather exaggerated than relieved by the character of the reaction to which it has conduced. Dissoluteness in one quarter is compensated by austerity equally in excess in another. . . . The picture is a true one of the effect on morals of laws or maxims too severe to be executed; and the action of the play exhibits the farther disorder and complication resulting from the mere revival of unamended statutes, that had never become obsolete but for their need of amendment, and can scarcely have a better fate again. . . . We are spectators of a receptacle of stagnant impurities in vehement ferment, and working through stages of decomposition, but the hope of ultimate purification is scarcely set forth so cheeringly as to compensate for the disagreeableness of what we witness."—LLOYD.

THE COMEDY OF ERRORS

Present play contains 5 Acts, 11 Scenes, 1758 lines

CAST OF CHARACTERS

SOLINUS, *Duke of Ephesus*
ÆGEON, *a merchant of Syracuse*
ANTIPHOLUS *of Ephesus,*⎫ *twin brothers, and sons to Ægeon and*
ANTIPHOLUS *of Syracuse,*⎭ *Æmilia*
DROMIO *of Ephesus,*⎫ *twin brothers, and attendants on the two*
DROMIO *of Syracuse,*⎭ *Antipholuses*
BALTHAZAR, *a merchant*
ANGELO, *a goldsmith*
First Merchant, friend to Antipholus of Syracuse
Second Merchant, to whom Angelo is a debtor
PINCH, *a schoolmaster*
ÆMILIA, *wife to Ægeon, an abbess at Ephesus*
ADRIANA, *wife to Antipholus of Ephesus*
LUCIANA, *sister to Adriana*
LUCE, *servant to Adriana*
A courtesan
Jailer, Officers, and other Attendants
SCENE: Ephesus

ACT I

Ægeon, a merchant of Syracuse, is condemned to death, in default of ransom, by the Duke of Ephesus for bringing traffic into the Ephesian port. Being requested by the Duke to give the cause of his visit to a hostile city, the prisoner states that he is on a quest for missing members of his family. Some years before, twin sons had been born to him and his wife Æmilia. At "that very hour and in the selfsame

67

inn" a poorer woman was also delivered of twin sons, which Ægeon had "bought and brought up to attend" his boys. Shortly afterwards the party had suffered shipwreck on a voyage to their Syracusian home. All had been rescued, but the husband was parted from the wife; and the twin sons and attendants were separated from their respective counterparts. Ægeon, with his younger son and servant, had been conveyed to Syracuse, where for eighteen years they dwelt without tidings of the other three. Finally Antipholus, his son, now well grown, had set forth in search of them, while Ægeon renewed his own quest. During seven years father and son had heard nothing of each other nor of the rest. All this Ægeon tells the Duke in explanation of his wanderings. Touched by the narrative, the Duke gives him further respite of a day in which to seek ransom.

Unknown to his father, Antipholus of Syracuse and his servant Dromio are even then visiting in Ephesus. Furthermore it so chances that his brother, whom he has not found and who is known as Antipholus of Ephesus, resides there in high favour with the Duke, and wedded to Adriana, a woman of rank. Dromio of Ephesus mistakes Antipholus of Syracuse for his master and delivers a message from Adriana to the effect that dinner is awaiting him.

ACT II

The servant having fled home beaten for his pains, Adriana herself arrives and persuades the bewildered Antipholus of Syracuse to come to dinner with her; for she also is deceived as to his identity. Dromio of Syracuse is put on guard at the gate with instructions to deny admittance to visitors during the repast.

ACT III

The real husband presently arrives at his door and is greatly astonished and incensed to find it barred against him, but is persuaded to retire to a public house and bide his time.

Meanwhile the false husband stoutly maintains that there is a mistake, and makes fair speeches to Luciana, sister of Adriana, rather than to Adriana herself. The two Dromios are suffering most of all from the comedy of errors, being continually confused, sent on the wrong errands and getting chastised.

ACT IV

The muddle of identities grows constantly more perplexing for both masters and servants. Tradesmen confuse the two Antipholuses. A gold chain made for the Ephesian is bestowed upon the Syracusian, and the Ephesian is arrested for refusing to pay the debt. The Syracusian and his servant believe themselves bewitched and prepare for speedy departure.

ACT V

They are forced to take refuge in a priory from the misguided merchants and Adriana. The abbess protects them. At this juncture the Duke arrives in company with officers conducting Ægeon to his execution. Adriana demands from the Duke custody of her husband, whom she believes to be demented and now sequestered in the priory. Charge and countercharge are made by conflicting witnesses until the joint appearance of both the Antipholuses and both the Dromios unravels the snarl. Antipholus of Ephesus is reconciled with his wife. Antipholus of Syracuse renews his suit with her sister Luciana. The old Ægeon is pardoned, and to the pleasure of greeting both his sons is added the delight of finding in the person of the abbess his long-lost wife Æmilia, while the two Dromios in the joy of meeting forget their woes and blows.

NOTES

The Comedy of Errors is mentioned by Meres in his "Palladis Tamia" (1598) among the six "excellent" comedies of Shakespeare. A still earlier mention is a reference in the "Gesta Grayorum" of 1594, to the effect that "a Comedy of Errors, like the Plautus his Menechmus, was played by the players" during the Christmas revels at Gray's Inn, in that year. Both plot and style indicate that this was one of Shakespeare's earliest plays, dating back to 1590 or 1591.

FIRST EDITION.   The earliest text is that of the First Folio of 1623, where it follows *Measure for Measure*. It is the shortest of all the plays.

SOURCES.   The "Menechmi" of Plautus, above-mentioned, was the inspiration of this play, the only question being as to whether Shakespeare obtained his inspiration directly, or through some intermediate piece. But he makes use only of Plautus's chief situation, the confusion arising from the mistaken identities of two men who strongly resemble each other. Further, the English dramatist creates the two Dromios, the mirth-provoking servants, and the episodes relating to Ægeon, as well as other personages and scenes not in the Latin version.

ACTION.   The action is confined to a single day. In the morning the aged Æeon is condemned to die by sunset; and the final scene shows him being led to execution. The classic unities of time and place are thus preserved in this play. The period is indefinite. Ephesus after the introduction of Christianity, or after the fourth century, is the nearest approximation.

SELECTED CRITICISM.   *"The Comedy of Errors* not only surpasses the 'Menechmi' in the greater complexity of its plot, its greater variety of incident, but also in its more generous treatment of human nature. Not that elaborately wrought-out characters are to be sought in it; for this, it must be remembered, is Shakespeare's most absolutely comic and almost farcical play, and in this particular class of work he never handled the incisive tool of an engraver, like Molière—his pencil runs galloping over the canvas with a light, fantastic touch; and this play is, moreover, one of his most youthful performances." —STAPFER.

MUCH ADO ABOUT NOTHING

✥ ✥ ✥

Present play contains 5 Acts, 17 Scenes, 2718 lines

CAST OF CHARACTERS

DON PEDRO, *Prince of Arragon*
DON JOHN, *natural brother to the Prince*
CLAUDIO, *a young lord of Florence*
BENEDICK, *a young lord of Padua*
LEONATO, *Governor of Messina*
ANTONIO, *brother to Leonato*
BALTHASAR, *attendant on Don Pedro*
CONRADE, ⎫
BORACHIO, ⎭ *followers of Don John*
FRIAR FRANCIS
DOGBERRY, *a constable*
VERGES, *a headborough*
A Sexton
A Boy
HERO, *daughter to Leonato*
BEATRICE, *niece to Leonato*
MARGARET, ⎫
URSULA, ⎭ *gentlewomen attending on Hero*
Messengers, Watch, Attendants, and others
SCENE: *Messina*

ACT I

Don Pedro, Prince of Arragon, comes on a visit to Leonato, Governor of Messina, accompanied by Benedick and Claudio, two young noblemen who have been serving with him in the wars. Between Benedick and Beatrice, Leonato's niece, there has been a merry war; so that "they never meet but there's

71

a skirmish of wit between them." On the occasion of this meeting they are true to their reputations for antagonism. Meanwhile, Claudio is attracted once again by Leonato's daughter, Hero. Don Pedro kindly offers to sue to the lady and her father in the young lord's behalf.

ACT II

A masquerade is given by Leonato in honour of his visitors. Don Pedro seizes the opportunity to woo Hero, giving her to think that he is Claudio. Don John, an evil-minded natural brother of the Prince, seeks to poison Claudio's mind by telling him that Don Pedro is wooing in his own behalf; and Claudio's spirits droop until the lady is actually promised him by her father. Seeing the small piece of villainy come to naught, Don John plots a much larger one. Benedick, on his part, fares badly at the masquerade. Beatrice flouts him so sadly that he is on the point of forsaking her society henceforth, when their friends, believing them to be well matched, decide upon a ruse to arouse their mutual affections. Benedick is made to overhear that Beatrice is in love with him.

ACT III

Beatrice is informed in the same fashion that Benedick loves her. Their hearts become more tender towards each other. Don John's evil plans are maturing against Hero and Claudio. He brings Claudio and Don Pedro beneath her window on the night before her wedding-day, and makes them believe that they are witnessing a meeting between her and some secret lover. The artifice is caused by Borachio, a follower of Don John, who addresses a waiting-maid as Hero; but the night is too dark to reveal the deception, and it would probably never have been discovered had not some blundering watchmen, by a happy chance, overheard Borachio telling of the adventure. They seize him and try to inform Leonato; but the latter, busied with the arrangements for the marriage, does not stop to listen to their rambling narrative.

ACT IV

Claudio believes Hero faithless, and repudiates her at the very moment of the nuptials. Hero swoons, and by the advice of a friar it is given out that she is dead. Beatrice will not believe her cousin guilty, and demands of Benedick—who has avowed his love—proof of his devotion in the shape of the life of Claudio, his friend.

ACT V

Leonato is in the depths of despair and humiliation over the evil report concerning his daughter. He upbraids Claudio and wishes to fight him. Benedick challenges Claudio. The testimony of the watchmen finally comes to light, revealing the plot of Don John and the innocence of Hero. Claudio sues for forgiveness, which the generous Leonato grants, on condition that Claudio wed a niece who is said to be much like Hero, but whose face he is not permitted to see until after the marriage ceremony has been performed. Claudio, who had promised any penance, willingly consents to this. His happiness, therefore, is made perfect when the masked lady proves to be Hero, whom he has been mourning as dead. While Beatrice and Benedick, although they find out the trick that has brought them together, are not sorry for it, but stop their bickerings with a kiss.

NOTES

Since Meres does not mention *Much Ado About Nothing* in his "Palladis Tamia" of 1598, and it appeared in Quarto form in 1600, the date of authorship may be assigned to 1599 or 1600. In style and treatment it belongs among the last of the comedies, about this period.

FIRST EDITIONS. The Quarto of 1600 bore this entry: "As it hath been sundry times publicly acted by the right honourable the Lord Chamberlain, his Servants." It was entered in the "Stationers' Register," August 23, 1600. The next known printing was that of the First Folio, of 1623, which follows the Quarto version with a few minor changes.

SOURCES. Three or four possible sources of inspiration have been mentioned for *Much Ado*. One is a story by Bandello, an Italian author. His twenty-second Novella tells of a certain Don Pedro of Arragon and a Lionato; the scene is Messina; and a lady maligned by the sudden appearance of a servant, swoons and is thought dead. Belleforest translated this story in his "Histoires Tragiques." The incident of the interrupted marriage is similar to the tale of Adriodante and Ginevra in "Orlando Furioso," by Ariosto; and another such situation appears in Book II, Canto 4, of Spenser's "Faerie Queene." A contemporary German version, "The Beautiful Phoenicia," has also been found; but Jacob Ayrer, the author, follows Bandello much more closely than does Shakespeare who invests the situation with his own characters and scenes.

ACTION. The time duration is clouded, but falls logically within four consecutive days. The period of the play is likewise uncertain, due to Shakespeare's indebtedness to an Italian setting. But treated solely as an English play of manners, Shakespeare's own time would be a satisfactory period.

SELECTED CRITICISM. "When we turn to the old stories upon which Shakespeare based his plays, we get, perhaps, a deeper impression of his essential originality than we should, were the plots wholly his own. . . . We see that the work grew from what the workman had within himself, and not merely from following what others had done before him. We see that the old story has been less worked into, than employed as the scaffolding of his dramatic structure. . . . The life and main interest of *Much Ado About Nothing* are due to characters which, so far as we know, were entirely original with Shakespeare, namely, Benedick and Beatrice, Dogberry and Verges."— CORSON.

LOVE'S LABOUR'S LOST

Present play contains 5 Acts, 9 Scenes, 2688 lines

CAST OF CHARACTERS

FERDINAND, *King of Navarre*

BIRON,
LONGAVILLE, } *Lords attending on the King*
DUMAIN,

BOYET,
MERCADE, } *Lords attending on the Princess of France*

DON ADRIANO DE ARMADO, *a fantastical Spaniard*
SIR NATHANIEL, *a curate*
HOLOFERNES, *a schoolmaster*
DULL, *a constable*
COSTARD, *a clown*
MOTH, *page to Armado*
A Forester
The PRINCESS *of France*

ROSALINE,
MARIA, } *Ladies attending on the Princess*
KATHARINE,

JAQUENETTA, *a country wench*
Lords, Attendants, and others

SCENE: *Navarre*

ACT I

Ferdinand, King of Navarre, and three of his lords, Biron, Longaville, and Dumain, forswear the society of women, and agree to lead austere lives, devoted to study, for three years. The court is barred against women by proclamation; and so stringent is the edict that Costard, a clown, who has been seen in company with Jaquenetta, a country wench, is ordered imprisoned for a week.

ACT II

The Princess of France, with her ladies, Rosaline, Maria, and Katharine, and other attendants approach the court of Navarre on an affair of state. Their contemplated visit had been discussed by the four gentlemen when the latter made their oath of retirement, and it had been agreed that the ladies must be received as befitted their station. The gentlemen, therefore, meet them courteously outside the gates, where the King causes pavilions to be erected for his royal guests, at the same time apologising that an oath prevents their maintenance in Navarre.

ACT III

Biron, who was the last to sign the oath, is the first to weaken. He falls in love with Rosaline, whom he had met before. He writes her a note and entrusts it for delivery to Costard, now at liberty. The clown has been freed by Armado, a Spaniard, in order that he may act as messenger for him to Jaquenetta.

ACT IV

Costard gets the notes of the Spaniard and the nobleman confused, delivering Armado's missive to Rosaline and Biron's to Jaquenetta. The Princess and her attendants derive much amusement from the Spaniard's fantastical message; while Jaquenetta, unable to decipher her letter, takes it to a schoolmaster, who, recognising Biron's name, and being aware of the edict, sends her with it to the King.

In the meantime, the King and his other two gentlemen respectively fall in love with the Princess and her other two ladies. Each lover being discovered by one or others of his friends in the act of writing love-verses is obliged to make confession of his passion—to the great scorn of Biron. But his triumph is short-lived, for Jaquenetta arrives with his missent letter, and Biron is forced to admit his own shortcomings. Since all are forsworn, they plan to make war upon the hearts of their feminine visitors.

ACT V

The ladies content themselves with the proffered hospitality outside the court. They pass their time in hunting and kindred outdoor pleasures. Presently all begin to receive letters and love-tokens from their several admirers, who visit them on one occasion in disguise. But the ladies, having got wind of their coming, also disguise themselves, and thus confuse the courtiers, so that each woos the wrong one and becomes the sport of her wit. The gentlemen retire and return in their proper habits, to find that the ladies have changed their favours, and to become dismayed at the blunders they commit. A masque is presented, but in the midst of it the Princess receives word of her father's death. She prepares for speedy departure. The King now sues openly for her hand, and also seeks the hands of her three ladies on behalf of his friends. The Princess is not yet ready to yield, but bids them wait a twelve-month and a day, and promises to give favourable answer at the expiration of that time, which is to be spent by the King in a hermitage, while she mourns her father. Her three ladies impose a like penance upon their lovers, who see, for the moment at least, their love's labour's lost.

NOTES

Several early references assist us in dating *Love's Labour's Lost*. Meres' "Palladis Tamia," of 1598, includes it with the then known plays of Shakespeare. Robert Tofte, in the same year, mentions it in his poem, "Alba." In this year, also, a Quarto edition of the play was published. Other references in the text would indicate that it was written between 1591 and 1594.

FIRST EDITIONS. The earliest printing was in a Quarto published in 1598, bearing the caption: "A pleasant conceited Comedie called

Loves Labours Lost. As it was presented before her Highness this last Christmas. Newly corrected and augmented by W. Shakespeare." This would seem to indicate that there was an earlier stage version. The First Folio, of 1623, evidently draws upon the Quarto for its version.

SOURCES. The plot of this play has not been traced to earlier sources, and is now believed to be Shakespeare's own.

ACTION. The action continues probably through two days; but the dramatist is not here concerned so much with the progress of events as with the dialogue and satire of the piece. It contains many references to contemporary events, such as the Queen's educational projects; King Henry of Navarre and his actions; Russian diplomacy; rural school life; the comic side of country life, such as blundering constables and pompous teachers; affectations of speech and dress in social life; etc.

SELECTED CRITICISM. *"Love's Labour's Lost* is one of the earliest of Shakespeare's dramas, and has many of the peculiarities of his poems, which are also the work of his earlier life. The opening speech of the King on the immortality of fame—and the nobler parts of Biron— display something of the monumental style of the *Sonnets,* and are not without their conceits of thought and expression. This connection is further enforced by the actual insertion of three sonnets and a faultless song. . . . There is merriment in it also, with choice illustrations of both wit and humor. . . . A dainty love-making is interchanged with the more cumbrous play."—WALTER PATER.

A MIDSUMMER NIGHT'S DREAM

✤ ✤ ✤

Present play contains 5 Acts, 13 Scenes, 2121 lines

CAST OF CHARACTERS

THESEUS, *Duke of Athens*
EGEUS, *father to Hermia* Helena Demetrius-Hermia—Lysander

LYSANDER, *in love with Hermia*
DEMETRIUS,

PHILOSTRATE, *Master of the Revels to Theseus*
QUINCE, *a carpenter*
SNUG, *a joiner*
BOTTOM, *a weaver*
FLUTE, *a bellows-mender*
SNOUT, *a tinker*
STARVELING, *a tailor*
HIPPOLYTA, *Queen of the Amazons, betrothed to Theseus*
HERMIA, *daughter to Egeus, in love with Lysander*
HELENA, *in love with Demetrius*
OBERON, *King of the Fairies*
TITANIA, *Queen of the Fairies*
PUCK, *or Robin Goodfellow*

PEASEBLOSSOM,
COBWEB, *Fairies*
MOTH,
MUSTARDSEED,

Other Fairies attending their King and Queen
Attendants on Theseus and Hippolyta

SCENE: *Athens, and a wood near it*

ACT I

Theseus, Duke of Athens, after conquering the Amazons in battle, is in turn conquered by the charms of their queen, Hippolyta, and plights troth with her. To speed the time until their wedding night, he orders amusements to be put on foot. Actuated by a spirit of loyalty, Bottom the weaver and other tradesmen prepare a play for the Duke.

Egeus, an Athenian, brings his daughter Hermia and her two suitors before Theseus, praying him to command Hermia to wed Demetrius. Hermia pleads to be allowed to marry the one she loves—Lysander. The Duke orders her to obey her father under penalty of death or of a conventual life. Hermia and Lysander bewail the harsh decree, and secretly agree to meet in a wood near by and flee to another country. They tell their plans to Helena, a jilted sweetheart of Demetrius, and she, to win back his love, goes straightway to inform him of the design.

ACT II

In the forest is great commotion among the fairies. King Oberon and Queen Titania are at odds. Oberon bids Puck procure a love-juice to pour upon Titania's eyelids when she is asleep, in order that she may love the first thing her waking eyes behold. Just then Oberon perceives Demetrius, who has sought out the trysting-place of Lysander and Hermia, only to meet Helena, much to his distaste. The lady's distress at her lover's coldness softens the heart of Oberon, who bids Puck touch Demetrius's eyes also with the love-juice, for Helena's sake, while he himself anoints the eyes of Titania. Meantime Lysander and Hermia arrive, and Puck in error anoints Lysander's instead of Demetrius's eyes; so that Lysander, happening to awake just as the neglected Helena wanders by, falls in love with her, to the abandonment of Hermia.

ACT III

This same enchanted spot in the forest happens to be the place selected by Bottom the weaver and his companions for the final rehearsal of their play. The roguish Puck passes that way while they are rehearsing, and decides to take a hand in the proceedings. He crowns Bottom with an ass's head, whereupon the other players disperse terror-stricken. Then he brings Bottom to Titania, whose enchanted gaze fixes upon the human ass as her heart's love.

Meantime the four lovers come into great bewilderment. Oberon finds that Puck has anointed the eyes of Lysander instead of those of Demetrius, which he himself now takes occasion to touch. When Demetrius awakes he sees his neglected Helena being wooed by Lysander. His own love for her returns, and he is ready to fight Lysander. Helena deems them both to be mocking her, while Hermia is dazed by the turn of affairs. The fairies interpose and prevent conflict by causing the four to wander about until they are tired, when they fall asleep. Puck repairs his blunder by anointing Lysander's eyes, in order to dispel the illusion caused by the love-juice.

ACT IV

Titania makes love to Bottom, till Oberon, whose anger has abated, removes the spell from her eyes. To Bottom is restored his natural form, and he rejoins his comrades in Athens. Theseus, on an early morning hunting-trip in the forest, discovers the four lovers. Explanations follow; the Duke relents and bestows Helena upon Demetrius and Hermia upon Lysander.

ACT V

A wedding-feast for three couples instead of one only is spread in Duke Theseus's palace. Thither come Bottom's players to present the comic tragedy of "Pyramus and Thisbe," which is performed in wondrous fashion. After the company retires for the night, the fairies dance through the corridors on a mission of blessing and good-will for the three wedded pairs.

NOTES

The date of composition of *A Midsummer Night's Dream* is uncertain, guesses ranging from 1593 to 1598. It was definitely mentioned in the latter year by Francis Meres in his "Palladis Tamia."

Attempts have been made to link up its first presentation with the marriage festivities of two of Shakespeare's patrons, Lord Southampton, and the Earl of Essex, but these are not conclusive. Textual references indicate either the years 1593 or 1594 as to probable time of writing.

FIRST EDITIONS. Two Quarto editions of this play appeared in 1600. One bore the inscription: "As it hath been sundry times publicly acted by the right honourable the Lord Chamberlain, his servants. Written by William Shakespeare. Imprinted at London for Thomas Fisher." The other Quarto bore the same title, but carried the name of James Roberts, instead of Fisher's. The editions are practically identical; and they are followed by the First Folio version, of 1623.

SOURCES. Many resemblances have been pointed out between the play and Chaucer's "Knight's Tale." The general situation is the same; and instead of Chaucer's gods of Olympus interfering with mortals' affairs we have the fairies. Oberon, the fairy king, is found in early English and French literature, and has been identified also with Alberich the dwarf of the "Nibelungenlied." Similarly, Titania and Puck were familiar and popular figures in superstition.

ACTION. Theseus states in the opening scene that "four happy days" are to elapse before their nuptial hour; but the action apparently takes only three days. The actual period of the play is as legendary as the plot. It is as easily suited to Merrie England in midsummer as to Greece.

SELECTED CRITICISM. "We have here an element of aristocratic distinction in the princely couple, Theseus and Hippolyta, and their court. We have an element of sprightly burlesque in the artisans' performance treated with genial irony and felicitous humor. And finally we have an element of supernatural poetry. . . . Puck and Pease-blossom, Cobweb and Mustard-seed . . . are the leading actors in an elfin play, a fairy carnival of inimitable mirth and melody. . . . This miracle of happy inspiration contains the germs of innumerable romantic achievements in England, Germany, and Denmark, more than two centuries later."—GEORG BRANDES.

THE MERCHANT OF VENICE

❖ ❖ ❖

Present play contains 5 Acts, 20 Scenes, 2590 lines

CAST OF CHARACTERS

ANTONIO, *a merchant of Venice*
BASSANIO, *friend to Antonio, and suitor to Portia*
SALANIO,
SALARINO,
GRATIANO, } *friends to Antonio and Bassanio*
SALERIO,
The DUKE *of Venice*
The PRINCE *of Morocco,*
The PRINCE *of Arragon,* } *suitors to Portia*
LORENZO, *in love with Jessica*
SHYLOCK, *a rich Jew*
TUBAL, *a Jew, friend to Shylock*
LAUNCELOT GOBBO, *a clown, servant to Shylock*
OLD GOBBO, *father to Launcelot*
LEONARDO, *servant to Bassanio*
BALTHASAR,
STEPHANO, } *servants to Portia*
PORTIA, *a wealthy gentlewoman*
NERISSA, *waiting-maid to Portia*
JESSICA, *daughter to Shylock*
Magnificoes of Venice, Officers of the Court of Justice, Jailer,
Servants to Portia, and other Attendants
SCENE: *Venice; Belmont—Portia's estate*

ACT I

Antonio, a merchant of Venice, has many dear friends who are
beholden to him for his good qualities; but most of all he loves

83

Bassanio, for whom he would make any sacrifice. Bassanio is in love with Portia, a wise and wealthy lady, but since he lacks worldly means wherewith to press his suit, he is constrained to borrow of his friend Antonio three thousand ducats ere he can visit her. Antonio's wealth is entirely represented, just then, by various ships at sea. However, he bethinks himself of a Jewish moneylender named Shylock, who lends him the money, under agreement that Antonio shall forfeit a pound of his flesh in default of payment on the day his bond falls due. The merchant signs the bond, thinking it a mere form of no significance.

ACT II

Although the Jew stipulates this forfeiture in seeming jest, he is nevertheless deeply in earnest, for he has long held a grudge against Antonio; and his rancour is strengthened at this juncture by the elopement of his only daughter, Jessica, with Lorenzo, another of Antonio's friends.

Before Portia's father died he made a curious provision in his will concerning her marriage, whereby her hand was to be given to the suitor who should choose that one of three caskets —respectively of gold, silver, and lead—containing her portrait. The choice of caskets baffles more than one.

ACT III

Bassanio arrives at Portia's house, and, much to her delight, rightly chooses the leaden casket. They plight their troth. But Bassanio's joy is overcast by the receipt of a letter from Antonio, advising him of the loss of the merchant's cargoes by shipwreck; and that the Jew is insistent upon the letter of his bond, Bassanio hastens back to his friend's succour. Portia privately resolves to be at the trial of Antonio.

ACT IV

Portia obtains from a kinsman the costume of a doctor of laws, investigates Antonio's case thoroughly, and appears at the trial before the Duke of Venice. In her disguise she is not recognised, even by her husband. She pleads the cause of Antonio with such eloquence and logic that Shylock not only loses his case, but also has his property confiscated for plotting against the life of a Venetian. The sentence against him is mitigated sufficiently to allow him to will his property to Jessica. Bassanio, overjoyed at his friend's victory, wishes to bestow upon the supposed lawyer the original sum of three thousand ducats as a fee. But Portia refuses it, and desires only a ring from Bassanio's finger. It is the ring she had given him when they exchanged vows, and he had sworn to keep it. He reluctantly gives it to the fair advocate.

ACT V

Portia's maid, Nerissa—newly wedded to Gratiano, a friend of Bassanio—had accompanied Portia to the trial in the guise of a clerk. She also had won back from her husband her engagement ring. When he returns with Bassanio to Portia's home, Nerissa feigns a very pretty quarrel with him for giving away the ring. Portia, overhearing the quarrel, points out her own husband as a worthier example of faithfulness, and affects much choler when his ring also is not to be found. A general explanation untangles the amusing snarl of events, and brings joy to every heart—even to that of the honest Merchant of Venice, who hears of the safe arrival of three of his ships.

NOTES

The Merchant of Venice is mentioned by Meres in his "Palladis Tamia," 1598; and in the same year it was entered in the "Stationers' Register" of London. A play, "Wily Beguiled," of 1596–7, contains an imitation of the moonlight scene between Lorenzo and Jessica. A still earlier date for Shakespeare's play may be indicated by an entry in Henslow's Diary, in 1594, which speaks of "the Venesyon Comodey" (Venetian Comedy) and may have reference to *The*

Merchant of Venice. The play may be dated anywhere between 1594 and 1598.

FIRST EDITIONS. Two Quarto editions appeared in 1600. One was "Printed by J. Roberts"; the other, "Printed by J. R., for Thomas Heyes." The two texts are practically identical. The First Folio of 1623 makes few changes from the earlier versions. Two other Quartos were printed, in 1637 and 1652.

SOURCES. On account of its involved plot several earlier plays or stories have been cited as Shakespeare's possible inspiration. One was a play called "The Jew," mentioned in 1579; another, the Italian story of "Il Pecerone," by Fiorentino, which contains the main incidents of a Jewish money-lender, the pound of flesh, and the lady Judge. The story of the three caskets has been traced to the "Gesta Romanorum," translated by Robinson. Marlowe's "Jew of Malta" must also be mentioned as a possible parallel. Still other possible sources have been discovered, as the themes of play were well-known; however, it remained for Shakespeare to fuse them together and give them immortality.

ACTION. The time consumed in the play is a few days over three months. The actual action, however, is seven or eight days. The period is indeterminate.

SELECTED CRITICISM. "In the exhibition of Shakespeare as an artist, it is natural to begin with the raw material which he worked up into finished masterpieces. For illustration of this no play could be more suitable than *The Merchant of Venice,* in which two tales already familiar in story form, have been woven together into a single plot. . . . The two leading personages of the one tale are the sources respectively of the Complication and Resolution in the other tale, which carry the Complication and Resolution of the drama as a whole. Thus simply does the movement of the whole play flow from the union of the two stories."—MOULTON.

AS YOU LIKE IT

❧ ❧ ❧

Present play contains 5 Acts, 22 Scenes, 2681 lines

CAST OF CHARACTERS

DUKE, *living in exile, in forest*
FREDERICK, *brother to the Duke, and usurper of his dominions*
AMIENS,
JAQUES, } *Lords attending on the banished Duke*
LE BEAU, *a courtier attending upon Frederick*
CHARLES, *wrestler to Frederick*
OLIVER,
JAQUES, } *sons to Sir Rowland de Boys*
ORLANDO,
ADAM,
DENNIS, } *servants to Oliver*
TOUCHSTONE, *a clown*
SIR OLIVER MARTEXT, *a Vicar*
CORIN,
SILVIUS, } *shepherds*
WILLIAM, *a country fellow, in love with Audrey*
A person representing Hymen
ROSALIND, *daughter to the banished Duke*
CELIA, *daughter to Frederick*
PHEBE, *a shepherdess*
AUDREY, *a country wench*
Lords, Pages, Attendants, and others
SCENE: *Oliver's house; Duke Frederick's court;*
the Forest of Arden

ACT I

A Duke of France, being dispossessed of his dominions by his younger brother, Frederick, retires to the neighbouring Forest

87

of Arden with a few of his faithful followers. His daughter Rosalind remains at her usurping uncle's court as companion for her beloved cousin, Celia. The two maidens witness a wrestling-match between the Duke's wrestler and Orlando, an unknown youth, in which the latter comes off victorious. Duke Frederick is pleased with the young man's prowess and is disposed to show him favour until he discovers Orlando to be the son of one of the banished Duke's friends. But Rosalind is delighted to hear of this connexion, since she has become favourably disposed towards Orlando.

The people are so fond of Rosalind because of her many accomplishments and for the sake of her father, that Duke Frederick in alarm banishes her also from the court. For love of her, Celia accompanies her cousin into exile.

ACT II

Rosalind assumes male attire and takes Celia to the Forest of Arden, where they purchase a country-place and reside as brother and sister. To the same wood comes Orlando, who has been forced to flee from home to escape the evil designs of his elder brother, Oliver, and who joins the company of the banished Duke.

ACT III

Rosalind is at first dismayed when she learns of the presence of Orlando in the forest, since she is dressed as a man. But presently her inventiveness leads her to make use of her disguise to test his affection for her, which had been aroused at the same time with her own for him on the day of the wrestling-match, and is now venting itself in sighs and in verses fastened at random on the trees. The lover is invited to visit the supposed youth and talk to him in the same manner that he would have talked to Rosalind. Orlando is glad to avail himself of this privilege, partly as an outlet to his pent-up sentiment, partly because Rosalind, even in man's garments, exerts a subtle fascination over him.

ACT IV

Orlando has the good fortune to rescue his brother Oliver from a serpent and a lioness, though becoming slightly wounded in an encounter with the beast. On finding him asleep, Orlando, remembering the wrongs at his hands, had been tempted to leave him to his fate, "but kindness, nobler ever than revenge," made him give aid. The two brothers are tenderly reconciled, and Oliver goes to acquaint Rosalind with Orlando's injury. Rosalind is not enough of a man to resist swooning at the tidings.

ACT V

Oliver and Celia no sooner see each other than they fall desperately in love and resolve upon speedy marriage. Rosalind, who is satisfied with the strength of Orlando's devotion, promises him that the wedding ceremony shall include him also, and that she will find means to bring his lady-love hither. She seeks out the banished Duke, her father, and obtains his consent, and thereupon appears before them in her proper attire, to the great delight of Orlando and the Duke. The wedding, instead of being a double, is a quadruple event, since it includes besides these two couples, a shepherd and his lass (who had foolishly been attracted by Rosalind in her male attire), and Touchstone, the court clown, who had followed the two maidens to the forest and there become enamoured of a country wench. The wedding-party is made all the happier by the tidings that the usurping Duke Frederick, while on his way to the forest with a large army for the purpose of exterminating the exiles, had met an aged hermit who had converted him "both from his enterprise and from the world." Struck with remorse, he restores the dukedom to his banished brother and seeks the life of a recluse, leaving the rightful Duke and his followers free to resume their former rank.

NOTES

As You Like It may be assigned to the year 1599 or 1600. There's no mention of it earlier. It quotes a line from Marlowe's "Hero and Leander," which appeared in 1598. An entry in the "Stationers' Register," London, in 1600 mentions the play, but states that its publication was "to be staied" (deferred).

FIRST EDITION.   For some reason this injunction held good until after Shakespeare's death; and the play was not printed until the First Folio of 1623.

SOURCES.   The plot seems to have been derived directly from a tale called "Rosalynde, Euphues' Golden Legacie," by Thomas Lodge, who in turn seems indebted to the "Tale of Gamelyn" which for a long time was ascribed to Chaucer. Shakespeare also makes mention of the Robin Hood legends. He may have got his suggestion for title from a line in Lodge's story, "If you like it so."

ACTION.   The scene of the play is "The Forest of Arden" or Ardennes in the northeast of France; but the dramatist was doubtless thinking of his own Arden in Warwick, and the feeling is more English than French. The time was also contemporary. The duration of action is ten days, not counting intervals mentioned between scenes.

SELECTED CRITICISM.   "Shakespeare, when he wrote this idyllic play, was himself in his Forest of Arden. He had ended one great ambition —the historical plays—and not yet commenced his tragedies. It was a resting place. He sends his imagination into the woods to find repose. Instead of the court and camps of England, and the embattled plains of France, here was this woodland scene, where the palm-tree, the lioness, and the serpent are to be found, possessed of a flora and fauna that flourish in spite of physical geographers. There is an open-air feeling throughout the play. The dialogue catches freedom and freshness from the atmosphere. 'Never is the scene within-doors, except when something discordant is introduced to heighten as it were the harmony.'"—EDWARD DOWDEN.

THE TAMING OF THE SHREW

Present play contains Induction, 2 Scenes,
5 Acts, 12 Scenes, 2300 lines

CAST OF CHARACTERS

IN INDUCTION

A LORD
CHRISTOPHER SLY, *a tinker*
Hostess, Page, Players, Huntsmen, and Servants

IN PLAY

BAPTISTA, *a rich gentleman of Padua*
VINCENTIO, *an old gentleman of Pisa*
LUCENTIO, *son to Vincentio, in love with Bianca*
PETRUCHIO, *a gentleman of Verona, a suitor to Katharina*
GREMIO,
HORTENSIO, } *suitors to Bianca*
TRANIO,
BIONDELLO, } *servants to Lucentio*
GRUMIO,
CURTIS, } *servants to Petruchio*
A Pedant
KATHARINA, *the Shrew*
BIANCA, } *daughters to Baptista*
Widow
Tailor, Haberdasher, and Servants attending on Baptista and
    Petruchio

SCENE: *Padua; and Petruchio's country house*

INDUCTION

A tinker named Christopher Sly is found in a drunken stupor
by a lord, who, to make sport, causes him to be conveyed to the

castle, clothed in the costliest apparel and placed in the richest bed. Upon awakening Sly finds himself surrounded by attendants who persuade him that he is a nobleman who for many years has been mentally deluded. And in his honour the following play is presented:—

ACT I

Baptista, a rich gentleman of Padua, has two daughters, Katharina and Bianca. The latter, because of her gentleness and charm, has numerous admirers. But her father refuses to listen to any of them until her elder sister is married, which event seems doubtful on account of Katharina's shrewish disposition. The several lovers of Bianca are in despair until the advent of a peculiar Veronese gentleman, Petruchio, whose hasty temperament seems well suited to the shrew.

Among Bianca's admirers is Lucentio, a native of Pisa, who decides to disguise himself and engage with Baptista as tutor for Bianca, giving over his proper name and rank to Tranio, his servant.

ACT II

Tranio sues as Lucentio for Bianca's hand, while the real Lucentio obtains the position as tutor, intending thus to try to win her covertly. In the meantime, Petruchio obtains Baptista's willing consent to his suit for Katharina, and woos her in singular fashion, overriding all her harshness and disdain with the abrupt declaration that they shall be married on the next Sunday.

ACT III

At the appointed time the wedding-party assembles without the bridegroom. But he appears after an interval clad in most incongruous apparel, which he persists in wearing to the church —despite the open disapproval of the party—declaring: "To me she's married, not unto my clothes." Immediately after the ceremony he departs for home with Katharina, not even tarrying for the wedding-feast, although his bride first entreats and then storms.

ACT IV

At his country-house, Petruchio treats Katharina rigorously while pretending to be assiduous in his care of her. She gets very little to eat, because he claims that the food is not cooked properly; and the new garments which have been ordered for her are rejected, although she is very well pleased with them. He is so harsh with the servants and so dogmatic in his statements, that his wife forgets her own arbitrary disposition in the desire to keep his temper even. Finally she becomes quite submissive to his will.

In Padua, the fictitious Lucentio obtains Baptista's consent to his suit for Bianca, while the real Lucentio succeeds in winning the lady. The presence of Lucentio's father becomes necessary, and Tranio presses an aged schoolmaster into service to play this part.

ACT V

At this juncture the real father arrives and encounters Tranio in his master's garments. Tranio must needs face it out to gain time for Lucentio, and is on the point of causing the arrest of the father, when Lucentio and Bianca arrive as man and wife. Mutual explanations follow, and the entire party gather at a banquet at Lucentio's home in Padua. Katharina and Petruchio are among the guests. After the feast is over and the ladies have withdrawn into another room, the gentlemen discuss obedience as a wifely virtue, and the opinion is expressed that Petruchio's wife must be "the veriest shrew of all." A wager is made, and to the general surprise, Katharina shows herself to be more gentle and yielding than Bianca or another bride there present.

NOTES

Considerable doubt exists both as to the date of *Taming of the Shrew*, and Shakespeare's entire authorship of the play. It is not mentioned by Meres, in his "Palladis Tamia" of 1598, unless an obscure allusion to a "Love's Labor's Won" refers to it. A play known as "A Shrew" was known to the stage as early as 1594, and it is believed that Shakespeare worked over this text. The date of his version is now believed to fall between 1596 and 1599.

FIRST EDITIONS. *The Taming of the Shrew* was first printed in the First Folio, of 1623. A Quarto, of 1631, reprinted this text, ascribing it to Shakespeare and stating that "it was acted by His Majesty's Servants at The Black Friars and the Globe." See note below under Sources, for earlier play.

SOURCES. Shakespeare's play was a thorough revision and improvement upon an earlier play published anonymously in 1594, "A pleasant conceited History called The Taming of A Shrew, as it was sundry times acted by the Earl of Pembroke his Servants." The text of this old play is still extant, and bears traces of more than one hand. It has been variously assigned to Marlowe, Greene, and Shakespeare; but the latter very greatly improved upon this relatively crude version in his finished play.

ACTION. The duration of the action is five or six days, with intervals suggested between scenes amounting to about two weeks. The induction conforms to England of Shakespeare's day; and the play proper to Italy of the same period.

SELECTED CRITICISM. "*The Taming of the Shrew* is almost the only one of Shakespeare's comedies that has a regular plot and downright moral. It is full of bustle, animation, and rapidity of action. It shows admirably how self-will is only to be got the better of by stronger will, and how one degree of ridiculous perversity is only to be driven out by another still greater. Petruchio is a madman in his senses; a very honest fellow who hardly speaks a word of truth and succeeds in all his tricks and impostures. He acts his assumed character to the life, with the most fantastical extravagance, with complete presence of mind, with untired animal spirits, and without a particle of ill-humor from beginning to end. The situation of poor Katherine, worn out by his incessant persecutions, becomes at last as pitiable as it is ludicrous."—HAZLITT.

ALL'S WELL THAT ENDS WELL

᚛ᚋ ᚛ᚋ ᚛ᚋ

Present play contains 5 Acts, 23 Scenes, 2809 lines

CAST OF CHARACTERS

KING *of France*
DUKE *of Florence*
BERTRAM, *Count to Rousillon*
LAFEU, *an old Lord*
PAROLLES, *a follower of Bertram*
STEWARD,
LAVACHE, *a clown,* } *servants to the Countess of Rousillon*
A Page
COUNTESS *of Rousillon, mother to Bertram*
HELENA, *a gentlewoman protected by the Countess*
A Widow of Florence
DIANA, *daughter to the Widow*
VIOLENTA,
MARIANA, } *Neighbours and Friends of the Widow*
Lords, Officers, Soldiers, and others, French and Florentine
SCENE: *Rousillon; Paris; Florence; Marseilles*

ACT I

Upon the death of a celebrated physician, his daughter Helena is given a home with the Countess of Rousillon, and she there falls desperately in love with the Countess' son, Bertram. His mother discovers the attachment, but is not displeased at it, for Helena, though poor and unknown, is a woman of much worth. Bertram, however, pays no heed to Helena, all his thoughts being turned to active service with the King of France, under whose protection he places himself after the death of his father. The King is suffering at this time from a

95

disease which has been pronounced incurable. Helena, hearing of the King's ailment, secures the Countess' permission to go and offer him a prescription left her by her father, who in his lifetime had become famous in the treatment of this and other diseases.

ACT II

Helena obtains an audience with the King, and after much persuasion induces him to try her remedy, exacting only a royal promise that, in the event of his being cured, the monarch shall bestow upon her the hand of a gentleman of her choosing. The cure is effected, and Helena chooses Bertram. The young Count disdains the match, but is forced to consent to the nuptials, under peril of the King's displeasure. But no sooner is the ceremony performed than Bertram departs for the Florentine war, without so much as kissing his bride.

ACT III

Helena is sent home to the Countess with a letter from Bertram to the effect that he will never recognise his wife until she can obtain possession of a ring, a family heirloom, from his finger, and become with child by him—to which conditions he subscribes a "never." He also renounces his family estates because of her, which so grieves the young woman that she departs, no one knows whither, in order not to keep him from his home.

In Florence, the Duke has made Bertram general of his horse, and the Count distinguishes himself in battle. Helena arrives in the city disguised as a pilgrim, and learns from a widow that Bertram has been making dishonourable proposals to her daughter, Diana. Helena, seeing an opportunity, through Diana, to work out the seemingly impossible conditions imposed by her husband, prevails upon the widow to aid her project.

ACT IV

In furtherance of Helena's plot, Diana obtains from Bertram the much-prized ring, and makes an assignation with him, at which, however, the woman he meets is not Diana, as he supposes, but Helena. Shortly afterward he returns to his mother, the Countess, who has been mourning Helena as dead.

ACT V

The King, at this time, is visiting at the Countess' palace in Rousillon. He becomes reconciled with Bertram—who had left the court surreptitiously—and is on the point of giving his consent to the young Count's marriage with another lady, when he detects a ring upon Bertram's finger which the monarch had formerly given Helena, and which she had placed upon her husband's finger in Florence. Bertram cannot give a satisfactory explanation of its presence, and the King suspects him of having laid violent hands upon his wife, when the lost Helena appears upon the scene, tells the truth concerning the Florentine assignation, and assures her husband that both his conditions have been fulfilled. The repentant Bertram gladly acknowledges her as his wife.

NOTES

There is no earlier positive record of *All's Well That Ends Well* than the First Folio of 1623. However, the allusion by Francis Meres, in his "Palladis Tamia," of 1598 to a comedy called "Love's Labor's Won" seems to link up with this play more nearly than to *The Shrew,* or one or two others. The play seems to be a blending of earlier with later styles; and critics now believe it to be the earlier "Love's Labor's Won," of about 1594, thoroughly revised by Shakespeare some ten years later.

FIRST EDITION. The First Folio, of 1623, as above stated, contains the earliest version now extant of *All's Well*. It is listed in the "Stationers' Register" of that year as of a play not previously entered.

SOURCES. The "Decameron" of Boccaccio contains a story closely paralleling the plot of *All's Well*. The principal character, Bertram, is Beltram in the Italian tale. The "Decameron" was rendered into

English by Paynter in his "Palace of Pleasure," 1566. Shakespeare made use of the central situation but added characters of his own and recast the piece in dramatic form.

ACTION. Eleven days cover the stage action, but the total elapsed time is reckoned as three months. The action moves by turns from Rousillon to Paris, Florence, and Marseilles. No particular period is indicated.

SELECTED CRITICISM. "The composition is not as successful as in most of the later comedies; several of the characters, such as the Countess and the Duke of Florence, Lafeu and Parolles, Violenta, and Mariana, do indeed take some external, but no internal part in the action. The reason of this unalterable and chief defect of the whole lies, it seems to me, in the subject matter of the piece, which is not exactly happily chosen; for it must necessarily be offensive to a finer sense of feeling when, in courtship, woman is the wooer."
—ULRICI.

TWELFTH NIGHT;

OR, WHAT YOU WILL

⚜ ⚜ ⚜

Present play contains 5 Acts, 18 Scenes, 2505 lines

CAST OF CHARACTERS

ORSINO, *Duke of Illyria*
SEBASTIAN, *brother to Viola*
ANTONIO, *a sea captain, friend to Sebastian*
A Sea Captain, friend to Viola
VALENTINE,
CURIO, } *gentlemen attending on the Duke*
SIR TOBY BELCH, *uncle to Olivia*
SIR ANDREW AGUECHEEK, *a foolish suitor to Olivia*
MALVOLIO, *steward to Olivia*
FABIAN,
FESTE, *a clown,* } *servants to Olivia*
OLIVIA, *a wealthy Countess*
VIOLA, *sister to Sebastian*
MARIA, *servant to Olivia*
Lords, Priests, Sailors, Officers, Musicians, and other Attendants
SCENE: *A city in Illyria, and the sea-coast near it*

ACT I

Sebastian and Viola, twins, are separated by shipwreck and each believes the other lost. Viola is cast ashore on the coast of Illyria. She thereupon dons male attire and obtains service as page with the Duke Orsino, who has been vainly suing for the hand of Olivia, a native lady. The Duke is pleased with the appearance of his new page and sends Viola to pay court for him to Olivia, which she does with so much gracefulness and eloquence that the lady becomes enamoured of the supposed youth instead of the master.

ACT II

Olivia sends favours and messages to Viola in which, naturally, the latter takes no interest. Viola, in turn, has conceived a passion for the Duke, which she is compelled to hide.

Olivia's steward, Malvolio, is so priggish and conceited that others of her household contrive a practical joke against him, sending him an anonymous love-letter which he is given to believe is from Olivia herself.

ACT III

Malvolio follows instructions contained in the letter, and behaves so ridiculously that his mistress believes him demented.

Meanwhile Olivia's love for Viola becomes so intense that she sues openly to the fictitious page, much to the latter's distress. Sir Andrew Aguecheek, a foolish suitor of Olivia's, is displeased at the favours shown the page, and in a spirit of bravado challenges Viola. Though both are eager to avoid the conflict, it is only averted by the arrival of officers.

ACT IV

Sebastian, Viola's brother, who was also cast up by the sea, comes to Illyria. He looks so much like his sister—especially since she is in men's garments—that Sir Andrew mistakes him for the page and renews the fight. This time he does not encounter a woman's shrinking spirit or weak arm, and he is soundly belaboured. Soon after, Olivia also meets Sebastian, supposes him to be Viola and reiterates her devotion. The delighted Sebastian returns love for love and they are secretly espoused before a priest.

ACT V

Olivia encounters Viola in company with the Duke and greets her by the title of husband. The bewildered page disavows the title, but the priest who performed the ceremony vouches for it. The Duke is much disgruntled that his favourite page should so abuse his confidence. Viola is meeting with general disfavour, when her brother Sebastian arrives on the scene, and the two who had thought each other dead are reunited. Olivia discovers that she has espoused the brother, after having wooed the sister, while the Duke finds that his attachment for his page becomes love when Viola resumes her feminine attire.

The secret of Malvolio's dementia is revealed, and he is released from the confinement in which he has been held.

NOTES

An entry in the Diary of a certain John Manningham, for 1601–2, states that on February 1 he witnessed "a play called Twelve Night, or What You Will." His description of the plot also fits Shakespeare's play. This is the earliest mention of *Twelfth Night;* and as it quotes from a song, "Farewell, dear heart" (1601), it may be definitely ascribed to 1601 or 1602.

FIRST EDITION. The play was first published, so far as now known, in the First Folio, of 1623.

SOURCES. Manningham's Diary alludes to the Italian play "Gl'Inganni" (The Cheats) in connection with *Twelfth Night.* There were two versions of this Italian play, by different authors, but with similar situations. Another still closer source is "The History of Apollonius and Silla," a story by Barnaby Rich, 1581, in a collection called "Farewell to the Military Profession." Rich in his turn was probably indebted to Bandello's "Novella." In brief, the situations were known as "stock," but it remained to Shakespeare to fuse them into classic form.

ACTION. The duration of time is three days, with an interval of three days between the first and second days. The scene is the coast of Illyria; the period of the play indeterminate. The play derives its name probably from the fact that it was first produced at the time of the Christmas Revels, or the Twelfth Night after.

SELECTED CRITICISM. "Malvolio, Sir Toby Belch, Sir Andrew Ague-cheek, Maria, and, above all, Viola, as they live in the comedy are Shakespearian to the heart. The framework of the play is essentially serious, a beautiful vein of poetic feeling runs through it, and, intermingled with these the most unforced and uproarious fun. In inventiveness in the comic type and in freedom in handling it, as well as in grouping of diverse materials and fusing them into a harmonious and captivating whole, this comedy was never surpassed by the dramatist."—HAMILTON W. MABIE.

THE WINTER'S TALE

❧ ❧ ❧

Present play contains 5 Acts, 15 Scenes, 2976 lines

CAST OF CHARACTERS

LEONTES, *King of Sicilia*
MAMILLIUS, *son to Leontes, and Prince of Sicilia*
CAMILLO,
ANTIGONUS, } *Lords of Sicilia*
CLEOMENES,
DION,
ROGERO, *a gentleman of Sicilia*
POLIXENES, *King of Bohemia*
FLORIZEL, *son to Polixenes, and Prince of Bohemia*
ARCHIDAMUS, *a lord of Bohemia*
An Old Shepherd, reputed father of Perdita
A Clown, son to the Shepherd
AUTOLYCUS, *a rogue*
A Mariner   *A Jailer*
HERMIONE, *Queen to Leontes*
PERDITA, *daughter to Leontes and Hermione*
PAULINA, *wife to Antigonus*
EMILIA, *a lady attending on Hermione*
MOPSA, } *shepherdesses*
DORCAS,
TIME, *as Chorus*
Lords, Gentlemen, Ladies, Officers, Servants, Shepherds and
  Shepherdesses
SCENE: *Sicilia; Bohemia*

ACT I

Polixenes, King of Bohemia, who is visiting his boyhood friend,
Leontes, King of Sicilia, becomes desirous of returning to his

own kingdom, and cannot be persuaded by his host to prolong his sojourn. Leontes then asks his queen, Hermione, to join her persuasions to his own. Her hospitable entreaties are so successful that Polixenes defers his departure. This slight incident is sufficient to arouse in Leontes a tempest of jealousy touching his queen's and his friend's mutual honour. He endeavours to prevail on a courtier named Camillo to poison Polixenes. The courtier argues unavailingly with his King on the injustice of his suspicions, but finally consents to prepare the cup; instead, however, he informs the guiltless and unsuspecting monarch of his danger, and flees with him to Bohemia.

ACT II

The flight confirms Leontes in his wild suspicions. He visits his wrath upon the innocent Hermione, causing her to be isolated in a dungeon, where she is shortly afterward delivered of a daughter. Paulina, a lady of the court, presents the babe to the King, but he disavows it, and orders it to be exposed in some remote desert place.

ACT III

The babe, who is named Perdita because she "is counted lost forever," is borne to a coast of Bohemia by a courtier who is afterwards destroyed by a bear, while the child is found by a poor shepherd, who rears it as his own.

Meanwhile Hermione, who has been brought to public trial, is completely vindicated by a Delphic oracle declaring: "Hermione is chaste; Polixenes blameless; Camillo a true subject; Leontes a jealous tyrant; his innocent babe truly begotten; and the King shall live without an heir, if that which is lost be not found." Leontes discredits the oracle and is punished by the tidings of the sudden death of Hermione and her only son. The monarch is brought by this stroke to realize the enormity of his offence. He repents and resolves to do daily penance.

ACT IV

Sixteen years pass by. In the court of Bohemia, Polixenes and his friend Camillo discuss the reported actions of the King's son Florizel, who of late has been paying assiduous attention to a shepherd's lass. In order to investigate the report they disguise themselves and visit the shepherd's cottage, where they find Florizel on the point of betrothing Perdita. The King wrathfully puts a stop to the betrothal, when the lovers resolve to flee the country. Camillo privately offers and prepares to conduct them to Sicilia, assuring them of a warm welcome on the part of Leontes.

ACT V

Florizel and Perdita are cordially received in Sicilia, but are closely pursued thither by Polixenes. At this juncture the clothing and jewels found with the infant sixteen years before are produced, thus establishing the identity of Perdita as daughter of Leontes. The joy of the two sovereigns at meeting again is redoubled by the prospect of uniting their children in marriage. One thing only is lacking to the perfect happiness of Leontes —the presence of his lost wife, whom he has never ceased to mourn. Thereupon Paulina invites the company to inspect a statue of Hermione. They pause spellbound at the triumph of art, for the supposed statue is so perfect as to seem animate. At last it actually stirs, and the enraptured Leontes finds that he is embracing not marble but his living wife Hermione, who, dwelling in retirement, has awaited the fulfilment of the oracle.

NOTES

The earliest direct reference to *The Winter's Tale* is in a "Book of Plays" by Dr. Simon Forman, who states that he witnessed a performance of it at the Globe Theater, May 15, 1611. He analyzes it as though it were a new play. Ben Johnson speaks of it in his "Bartholomew Fair" (1612–14). It is also recorded among the Court Revels as having been performed November 5, 1611. In style also it belongs to the latest comedies, 1610–11.

FIRST EDITION. The first printed version was that of the First Folio, of 1623. It was also officially entered this same year.

SOURCES. Robert Greene, a contemporary of Shakespeare's, wrote a tale in 1588, which bore the title, "Pandosto, the Triumph of Time," and which was closely followed in theme by Shakespeare. The novel was quite popular, no less than fourteen editions being printed. Four out of five of the acts of the play follow the novel, but with the names of the characters changed. The fifth act is the dramatist's own, but may have been suggested by the "Alcestis" of Euripides.

ACTION.   The classic unities of time and place (adhered to in *The Tempest,* another late comedy) are entirely lacking here. The place of action shifts hundreds of miles between two scenes, and the time jumps forward sixteen years between two acts. Eight days are actually represented on the stage. The period also is indeterminate, being marked by several curious anachronisms.

SELECTED CRITICISM. "Shakespeare has treated Greene's narrative in the way he has usually dealt with his bad originals—he has done away with some indelicacy in the matter, and some unnatural things in the form; he has given a better foundation to the characters and course of events; but to impart an intrinsic value to the subject as a whole, to bring a double action into unity, and to give to the play the character of a regular drama by mere arrangements of matter and alteration of motive was not possible. . . . Shakespeare, therefore, began upon his theme in quite an opposite direction. . . . He overleaped all limits, mixing up together Russian emperors and the Delphic oracle and Julio Romana, chivalry and heathendom, ancient forms of religion and whitsuntide pastorals."
—GERVINUS.

CYMBELINE

❧ ❧ ❧

Present play contains 5 Acts, 27 Scenes, 3274 lines

CAST OF CHARACTERS

CYMBELINE, *King of Britain*
CLOTEN, *son to the Queen by a former husband*
POSTHUMUS LEONATUS, *a gentleman, husband to Imogen*
BELARIUS, *a banished Lord, disguised under the name of Morgan*
GUIDERIUS,⎫ *sons to Cymbeline, disguised under the names of*
ARVIRAGUS,⎰ *Polydore and Cadwal, supposed sons to Morgan*
PHILARIO, *friend to Posthumus,*⎫ *Italians*
IACHIMO, *friend to Philario,*⎰
CAIUS LUCIUS, *General of the Roman forces*
PISANIO, *servant to Posthumus*   CORNELIUS, *a physician*
A Roman Captain   *Two British Captains*
A Frenchman, friend to Philario
Two Lords of Cymbeline's court
Two Gentlemen of the same
Two Jailers
QUEEN, *wife to Cymbeline*
IMOGEN, *daughter to Cymbeline by a former Queen*
HELEN, *a lady attending on Imogen*
Lords, Ladies, Roman Senators, Tribunes, Soothsayer, Dutch-
    man, Spaniard, Musicians, Officers, Captains, Soldiers,
    Messengers, and other Attendants
Apparitions
                SCENE: *Britain; Rome*

ACT I

The displeasure of Cymbeline, King of Britain, is aroused
against Posthumus, a gentleman who has presumed to wed

the King's daughter, Imogen, and Posthumus is sent into exile. Arriving in Rome, he encounters an evil-minded Italian named Iachimo, who casts aspersions on the chastity of all women, and offers to wager that he will work the dishonour of Imogen. Posthumus has such confidence in his wife's integrity that he consents to the trial. Iachimo proceeds to the British court and, not succeeding in his open overtures with Imogen, has recourse to stealth.

ACT II

He gains admittance to her bedchamber by having himself carried there in a trunk. While she sleeps he takes off a bracelet from her arm and obtains a mental description of her room and person. Armed with this circumstantial evidence, he returns to Posthumus and is enabled thereby to convince him of Imogen's guilt.

ACT III

The misguided husband sends an order to his faithful servant Pisanio to put Imogen to death; which order is disregarded by Pisanio, who instead induces Imogen to disguise herself in male attire and go in search of Posthumus. By this flight she is likewise enabled to escape the malice of the Queen, her stepmother, and the disagreeable attentions of the Queen's son, Cloten. While traversing the mountainous country of Wales, Imogen by chance pauses faint and hungry before a cave wherein dwells Belarius, a banished nobleman, disguised as a peasant, who, in revenge for his unjust banishment, had abducted the King's two sons some twenty years before. The princes, now fully grown, though ignorant of their descent and also of the identity of the stranger, are strongly attracted to Imogen by the subtle tie of blood, and entertain her hospitably.

ACT IV

Cloten arrives before the cave in pursuit of Imogen, and is slain in a duel by one of the princes. His headless body is left lightly covered with leaves and flowers. Imogen, having on her person a poison prepared by the Queen, swallows it under the belief that it is a soothing cordial, and immediately falls into a deep sleep resembling death. The heart-broken princes lay her body beside that of Cloten. Shortly after she awakes from her stupor and mistakes the headless body for that of her lost lord Posthumus. In her despair she seeks service as page with a Roman general who is just then invading Britain.

ACT V

With the Roman army come Iachimo and Posthumus. A battle is fought against the forces of Cymbeline. Posthumus in the garb of a peasant fights valorously for Britain. Belarius and the two princes also render signal service to Cymbeline, aiding him to rout the Romans. The service paves the way for a reconciliation between Belarius and the King, in which the former reveals the identity of the two long-lost princes.

Amongst the prisoners taken are Iachimo and Imogen, the supposed page. The Italian makes a confession of his villainy, and Imogen is restored to Posthumus, whom the King receives again into favour. The malicious Queen dies in despair at the frustration of her designs.

NOTES

No exact date can be assigned for *Cymbeline*. Dr. Simon Forman, in his "Book of Plays," mentions having seen three Shakesperean plays at the Globe Theater, about 1610 and 1611. *Cymbeline* is one of them, but no date is given, as in the case of *The Winter's Tale*. Internal evidence places it among the final comedies, of about 1609–10.

FIRST EDITION. The First Folio, of 1623, was the first printed version; the editors there placing it among the tragedies, and so calling it. But the play does not have a tragic ending, and is now classed as a romantic comedy. The text is somewhat unsatisfactory in its misprints and obscure passages, and seems to lack the dramatist's final revision.

SOURCES. In their search for possible sources, critics divide this play into three themes: (1) Historical. Holinshed's "Chronicles" supply the names of the British King and his two sons, with a few meagre happenings of history. (2) Imogen. Derived from Boccaccio's "Decameron"—one of the second day stories of Bernabo of Genoa; or possibly from another current tale of "The Four Merchants, or the Virtuous Wife." Still another similar tale was "Westward for Smelts." (3) Imogen's adventures—which are not found in any of the above sources, but recall the fairy tale of "Snow White."

ACTION. As to historical period, Cymbeline is supposed to have reigned in England about the time of Christ. The time is legendary. The duration of action is about twelve days, with several intervals between scenes.

SELECTED CRITICISM. "The play is not merely a series of beautiful pictures, of interesting episodes, such as we are accustomed to find in the productions of dramatists of less renown. Here, as elsewhere in Shakespeare, everything is subservient to the development of character. From this point of view every scene contributes its share to the denouement, nor is there any falling off observable in the power of the artist. . . . He has put forth all his strength on the central figure of the drama, the matchless Imogen. . . . In her is to be found everything that makes woman lovable, and there is no situation in which she is placed which does not reveal some fresh beauty in her character."—EVANS.

CORIOLANUS

Present play contains 5 Acts, 29 Scenes, 3318 lines

CAST OF CHARACTERS

CAIUS MARCIUS, *afterwards* CAIUS MARCIUS CORIOLANUS, *a Roman General*

TITUS LARTIUS,
COMINIUS, } *Generals against the Volscians*

MENENIUS AGRIPPA, *friend to Coriolanus*

SICINIUS VELUTUS,
JUNIUS BRUTUS, } *Tribunes of the People*

YOUNG MARCIUS, *son to Coriolanus*

A Roman Herald

TULLUS AUFIDIUS, *General of the Volscians*

Lieutenant to Aufidius

Conspirators with Aufidius

A Citizen of Antium

Two Volscian Guards

VOLUMNIA, *mother to Coriolanus*

VIRGILIA, *wife to Coriolanus*

VALERIA, *friend to Virgilia*

Gentlewoman, attending on Virgilia

Roman and Volscian Senators, Patricians, Ædiles, Lictors, Soldiers, Citizens, Messengers, Servants to Aufidius, and other Attendants

SCENE: *Rome and its environs; Corioli and its environs; Antium*

ACT I

After the expulsion of the Tarquins from Rome ensues a famine, which is relieved by a free distribution of corn. This allowance encourages the plebeians to make further demands upon the patricians, from whom they ask corn henceforth at their own price. As a concession, five tribunes elected by themselves are allowed to represent them—two of whom, Sicinius Velutus and Junius Brutus, are demagogues, and, therefore, opposed to Caius Marcius, a high-minded nobleman, who will not curry favour with the populace. Naturally Marcius is unpopular, in spite of a splendid military record; but war breaking out at this time with the Volscians, he is enabled to regain popular favour and win fresh glory. He does such heroic deeds at Corioli, that the other two generals and all the army enthusiastically greet him with the title of Coriolanus.

ACT II

A triumph is accorded Coriolanus on his return to Rome; and the senate elects him consul. But he must also obtain the "voice of the people" through open solicitation. To the proud, reserved man the task is a hard one, and his overtures to the citizens are made so awkwardly, that although he is privately given their voice, they are discontented, and it needs only the influence of Sicinius and Brutus to cause them to repent their decision.

ACT III

When it comes to the open choice of Coriolanus for consul the fickle people disavow him. His ire is aroused, causing him to make vehement statements against the popular rights. The utterances are gladly seized upon and made use of by the two tribunes, who condemn him to exile, by decree of the people.

ACT IV

Deeply wounded at the ingratitude, and thirsting for revenge, Coriolanus goes to Antium where dwells his Volscian foe, Tullus Aufidius. He makes peace with that general, who is delighted to acquire the aid of the stoutest arm in Italy just at a time when a new campaign against the Romans is being planned, though he soon after begins to dread Coriolanus's power. The expedition proceeds against Rome, to the utter dismay of the tribunes and their adherents.

ACT V

The Roman forces being powerless to cope with the invasion, send peaceful embassies to Coriolanus, now encamped with Aufidius near the capital city. Though Coriolanus's stanchest friends are sent to him, he remains obdurate until his well-beloved mother and wife come to make powerful entreaty. He cannot withstand their prayers, and raises the siege without striking a blow. The Volscian army returns to Antium. Coriolanus attempts to justify his conduct to the lords of the city, and doubtless would succeed on account of his numerous conquests, did not Aufidius use his final action before Rome for a text to charge him with treachery. In the ensuing dispute some conspirators hired by Aufidius assassinate Coriolanus.

NOTES

No definite date can be assigned to *Coriolanus*. No references by other contemporaries are extant, and critics have been forced back upon the text itself for data. The years 1608–1610 seem most probable as to time of authorship.

FIRST EDITION. The play was first published in the First Folio, of 1623, where it was included among the Tragedies. It is mentioned in the "Stationers' Register," London, in the same year as one of sixteen plays not previously entered.

SOURCES. In 1579, Sir Thomas North published an English version of Plutarch's "Lives." This supplied Shakespeare not only with the groundwork of the story of *Coriolanus*, but also with much of the language of the text, the dramatist merely rewriting the prose into blank verse.

ACTION. Eleven days are represented on the stage. The intervals between scenes indicate "a period of about four years, commencing with the secession to the Mons Sacer in the year of Rome, 262, and ending with the death of Coriolanus, A. U. C. 266." (New Shakes. Soc. Transactions.)

SELECTED CRITICISM. "There is more unity in the tragedy of *Coriolanus* than in either of the other Roman plays; yet, grand and powerful as it is, its tragical interest is less than that of *Julius Cæsar,* and its poetical merit less than that of *Antony and Cleopatra.* There is something hard about it, both in sentiment and in style. The delineation of social and personal pride is not a subject to evoke much sympathy or emotion, and although it may in its course reach sublime heights, its sublimity is wholly independent of moral greatness. Of all Shakespeare's greater works, this is the most difficult to construe; the unintelligibility of several passages is doubtless due to some corruption of the text, but besides this, the general style is exceedingly obscure, and overloaded with metaphorical and elliptical expressions."—STAPFER.

KING JOHN

Present play contains 5 Acts, 17 Scenes, 2569 lines

CAST OF CHARACTERS

KING JOHN *of England*
PRINCE HENRY, *son to the King*
ARTHUR, *Duke of Bretagne, nephew to the King*
WILLIAM MARESHALL, *Earl of Pembroke*
GEFFREY FITZ-PETER, *Earl of Essex*
WILLIAM LONGSWORD, *Earl of Salisbury*
ROBERT BIGOT, *Earl of Norfolk*
HUBERT DE BURGH, *Chamberlain*
ROBERT FAULCONBRIDGE, *son to Sir Robert Faulconbridge*
PHILIP, *natural half-brother to Robert Faulconbridge*
JAMES GURNEY, *servant to Lady Faulconbridge*
PETER *of Pomfret, a prophet*   PHILIP, *King of France*
LEWIS, *the Dauphin*   LYMOGES, *Duke of Austria*
CARDINAL PANDULPH, *the Pope's Legate*
MELUN, *a French Lord*
CHATILLON, *Ambassador from France to King John*
QUEEN ELINOR, *mother to King John*
CONSTANCE, *mother to Arthur*
BLANCH, *of Spain, niece to King John*
LADY FAULCONBRIDGE
*Lords, Ladies, Citizens of Angiers, Sheriff, Heralds, Officers,
Soldiers, Messengers, and other Attendants*
SCENE: *England; France*

ACT I

After the death of Richard Cœur-de-Lion, the throne of England is seized by his brother John from the feeble grasp of their nephew Arthur, the rightful heir. King Philip of France supports the claims of Arthur, and menaces England with war; whereupon King John plans an invasion of France, and chooses as one of his generals a natural son of Cœur-de-Lion, whom he creates Sir Richard Plantagenet.

ACT II

The English troops encounter the French forces before the city of Angiers—an English possession, which, however, refuses to open its gates to either king till the succession of the English throne be determined upon. The two sovereigns fight a battle without decisive result, and afterwards propose a treaty of peace. A niece of John is given in marriage to the French Dauphin. The treaty results in an acquisition of English territory on the part of Philip, who is thereby disaffected to the cause of Arthur.

ACT III

King John refuses to bow to the authority of the Pope, and the latter excommunicates him. The papal legate incites Philip to break the treaty. War is resumed. The French are defeated in a general engagement, and Arthur is taken prisoner by his uncle, who gives secret orders that he be put to death.

ACT IV

Upon the return of John to England, Hubert, a courtier, is instructed to burn out Arthur's eyes, but the young prince's entreaties so soften Hubert's heart that he ventures to disobey the cruel mandate. Soon after, Arthur attempts to escape from the castle where he is confined, by leaping from the battlements. The leap kills him, and his mangled body is found by some discontented nobles. They believe him to have been murdered by the King's command, and are confirmed in their purpose of deserting John and joining their strength with that of the Dauphin, who, armed with papal approval, is invading England.

ACT V

The timid heart of John yields at this evidence of the Pope's wrath and power. He surrenders his authority to the papal legate, thinking thus to arrest the French invasion. But the Dauphin, urged by successes and claiming the English throne through his wife, continues to press forward. The English troops are mustered by Plantagenet, who valiantly battles with the French. The issue of the fray remains in doubt, each side having met with severe losses through outside and natural causes. The English nobles who had joined with the Dauphin now desert him, and he is disposed to terms of peace, which are willingly listened to by the enfeebled English. During the battle John has been removed in a state of illness to an abbey, where he is poisoned by a monk. Upon his death, his son Henry III ascends the throne.

NOTES

King John is listed by Francis Meres in his "Palladis Tamia," 1598. It therefore antedates that year, and textual evidence places it with a group of historical plays of about the year 1595.

FIRST EDITION. The earliest publication of *King John* now known is the First Folio, of 1623. The editors were guided by chronological sequence, and therefore placed this play at the head of the Histories.

SOURCES. This is a recast of an earlier play entitled "The Troublesome Reign of John, King of England," printed in 1591; which in turn may have been inspired by a play by Bishop Bale, "King John," published about 1558. Shakespeare follows the main facts of "The Troublesome Reign," merely compressing, adapting, and rewriting to suit his own needs. A later edition of "The Reign" places his name on the title-page, but it is clearly not his, but rather the work of two or three collaborators of an earlier school.

ACTION. The historical period covers the whole of King John's reign (1199–1216). It is noteworthy, however, in omitting reference to the signing of the Magna Charta, due doubtless to a similar omission in "The Troublesome Reign." The duration of action as shown on the stage is seven days, with intervals suggested between scenes.

SELECTED CRITICISM. "The play marks the transition from the chronicle play to the true drama; in which incidents and characters are selected for their dramatic significance, a dramatic motive introduced, dramatic movement traced, and a climax reached. The older playwrights, dealing with the events of a whole reign, would have given the play an epical or narrative quality; Shakespeare selected, compressed, foreshortened, and grouped events and figures in such a way as to secure connected action, the development of character, and a final catastrophe which is impressive, if not intrinsically dramatic. . . . The play has no hero, and is not free from the faults of the long line of dramas from which it descended and to which it belongs, but Shakespeare's creative energy is distinctly at work in it."—MABIE.

KING RICHARD THE SECOND

Present play contains 5 Acts, 19 Scenes, 2739 lines

CAST OF CHARACTERS

KING RICHARD *the Second of England*
JOHN OF GAUNT, *Duke of Lancaster,*
EDMUND OF LANGLEY, *Duke of York,* } *uncles to the King*
HENRY, *surnamed* BOLINGBROKE, *Duke of Hereford; son to John
    of Gaunt; afterwards* KING HENRY *the Fourth*
DUKE OF AUMERLE, *son to the Duke of York*
THOMAS MOWBRAY, *Duke of Norfolk*
DUKE OF SURREY
EARL OF SALISBURY
LORD BERKELEY
BUSHY,
BAGOT, } *servants to King Richard*
GREEN,
EARL OF NORTHUMBERLAND
HENRY PERCY, *surnamed* HOTSPUR, *his son*
LORD ROSS
LORD WILLOUGHBY
LORD FITZWATER
Bishop of Carlisle
Abbot of Westminster
Lord Marshal
SIR STEPHEN SCROOP
SIR PIERCE, *of Exton*
Captain of a Band of Welshmen
QUEEN *to King Richard*
DUCHESS OF YORK
DUCHESS OF GLOUCESTER
Lady attending on the Queen

Lords, Heralds, Officers, Soldiers, two Gardeners, Keeper, Messenger, Groom, and other Attendants
SCENE: *England and Wales*

ACT I

Henry, surnamed Bolingbroke, eldest son of John of Gaunt, Duke of Lancaster, in the presence of King Richard II charges Thomas Mowbray, Duke of Norfolk, with misappropriation of public funds and high treason. The King permits the two lords to meet in the lists to settle their dispute by deadly combat. But at the appointed time, when the charge has been sounded, the King interposes and sentences Norfolk to exile for life, while Bolingbroke is banished for six years. Richard is secretly glad thus to rid himself of Bolingbroke, whose popularity with the masses has become a menace to the throne.

ACT II

Shortly after his son's banishment, John of Gaunt dies; but has time upon his death-bed to reproach King Richard for mortgaging his realm, which the indigent monarch had done in order to raise funds for an Irish campaign. When Gaunt is dead, Richard unjustly confiscates his estates. Incensed by the wrong, Bolingbroke makes of this a pretext for invading England during the King's absence on his campaign. Many powerful nobles flock to the standard of Bolingbroke, who announces that he is but come after his inheritance of Lancaster.

ACT III

Learning of the ominous rebellion, King Richard returns from Ireland. To him Salisbury reports the disaffection of the Welsh, who had dispersed, believing the King to be dead. Richard's forces are not strong enough to cope with Bolingbroke, so he is driven to hold parley with the latter in Flint Castle, Wales. Bolingbroke artfully protests his loyalty and merely pleads that his sentence of exile be repealed and his patrimony be restored to him. The powerless monarch yields, and proceeds to London in the company of his formidable subject.

ACT IV

Arrived there, Bolingbroke reveals his true purpose of forcing Richard to abdicate in his favour. Richard is confronted with a list of formal charges and the crown is taken from him, after which he is ordered to be conveyed to the Tower.

ACT V

Bolingbroke rides through London in triumph and is hailed as King Henry IV. One of his first acts of clemency is to pardon the son of the Duke of York, who has been found guilty of treason. Richard is removed to the Castle of Pomfret instead of to the Tower, and is put to death with the connivance of the usurping King Henry IV, who promises, as an act of penance, to make a pilgrimage to the Holy Land.

NOTES

King Richard the Second was published in Quarto form, in 1597. Two years previously, Daniel's "Civil Wars" appeared, which contained some striking parallels. The play may therefore be assigned to the year 1595 or 1596.

FIRST EDITIONS. As above stated, the first appearance in book form was a Quarto, of 1597, stating, "As it hath been publicly acted by the Right Honorable the Lord Chamberlain his Servants." Shakespeare's name was not on the title page, but a Second Quarto appeared the same year, bearing his name. The play was entered in the "Stationers' Register" also in 1597. A Third Quarto came out in 1608, with a few additions. A Fourth Quarto, 1615, reprinted this, and was evidently the version of the First Folio of 1623.

SOURCES. Holinshed's "Chronicles" were followed closely in this play, both for groundwork and chief characters. Though there were other histories extant, such as Hall's "Chronicles" and Froissart's "Chronicles," it is Holinshed who furnishes the dramatist's inspiration. However, all these histories were merely "dry bones" of fact, which were clothed with life and romance by the playwright.

ACTION. The historic period extends from April, 1398, to March, 1400. The time indicated on the stage is two weeks.

SELECTED CRITICISM. "The spirit of patriotic reminiscence is the all-permeating soul of this noble work. It is, perhaps, the most purely historical of Shakespeare's dramas. There are not in it, as in the others, characters introduced merely for the purpose of giving a greater individuality and realness, as in the comic parts of *Henry the Fourth,* by presenting, as it were, our very selves. Shakespeare avails himself of every opportunity to effect the great object of the historic drama, that, namely, of familiarizing the people to the great names of their country, and thereby of exciting a steady patriotism, a love of just liberty, and a respect for all those fundamental institutions of social life which bind men together."—COLERIDGE.

THE FIRST PART OF

KING HENRY THE FOURTH

❧ ❧ ❧

Present play contains 5 Acts, 19 Scenes, 2999 lines

CAST OF CHARACTERS

KING HENRY *the Fourth of England*
HENRY, *Prince of Wales,*
JOHN, *of Lancaster,* } *sons to the King*
EARL OF WESTMORELAND
SIR WALTER BLUNT
THOMAS PERCY, *Earl of Worcester*
HENRY PERCY, *Earl of Northumberland*
HENRY PERCY, *surnamed* HOTSPUR, *his son*
EDMUND MORTIMER, *Earl of March*
RICHARD SCROOP, *Archbishop of York*
ARCHIBALD, *Earl of Douglas*
OWEN GLENDOWER
SIR RICHARD VERNON
SIR JOHN FALSTAFF
SIR MICHAEL, *friend to the Archbishop of York*
POINS   GADSHILL
PETO   BARDOLPH
LADY PERCY, *wife to Hotspur, and sister to Mortimer*
LADY MORTIMER, *daughter to Glendower, and wife to Mortimer*
MISTRESS QUICKLY, *hostess of a tavern in Eastcheap*
Lords, Officers, Sheriff, Vintner, Chamberlain, Drawers, two
Carriers, Travellers, and Attendants
SCENE: *England*

ACT I

After Bolingbroke has deposed Richard II of England and
ascended the throne as Henry IV, he seeks a time of peace

to go on his long-contemplated crusade; but is dissuaded from his purpose by the news of uprisings and battles in Wales and Scotland. The Scots under the command of Douglas make an incursion but at Holmedon suffer defeat by the English forces of Northumberland's son, Henry Percy, the famous Hotspur of history. The King no sooner hears of the victory than he demands the prisoners. These Hotspur is unwilling to give up unless the King will ransom Percy's kinsman, Mortimer. They quarrel; and Hotspur sends his prisoners home without ransom and plots with both the Scots and the Welsh to overthrow the sovereign he had so recently helped to seat.

ACT II

The madcap pranks and dissolute companions of the Prince of Wales are a source of anxiety to his father. The Prince's boon companion is a corpulent warrior, Sir John Falstaff, who wars mainly with his tongue and the wine-bottle. Falstaff and three companions rob some travellers on the highway, and are set upon in turn by the Prince and one comrade in disguise, who put them to flight; and when later Falstaff would boast of his imaginary encounter with innumerable foes the Prince has a hearty laugh at his expense. His merriment is interrupted by news from the court of Hotspur's rising in the North.

ACT III

The Prince immediately awakes to a sense of his responsibilities, assures his royal father of his intention to be more worthy of the title of Prince, and is entrusted with a wing of the army that is proceeding against Hotspur. The Prince procures for Falstaff a small command of infantry.

ACT IV

Hotspur is disadvantaged by the non-arrival of bodies of troops counted on by him from his father and from Wales. Nevertheless he encamps at Shrewsbury, and resolves on instant battle when the royal troops approach.

ACT V

The King leads his army in person, and before Shrewsbury holds parley with the rebels, to whom he promises pardon if they will lay down their arms. But Hotspur is misinformed of the terms of parley and gives battle. In the spirited and decisive contest the rebels are defeated. Hotspur is slain by the Prince— though credit for the death is claimed by the rascally Falstaff —and King Henry begins to realize the true worth of his valiant son.

NOTES

There is abundant evidence going to show that the *First Part of King Henry the Fourth* was written in 1596 or 1597. It was published in 1598, and Meres also mentions it then. The opening lines of the play are believed to refer to the Spanish expedition of 1596. An allusion to the "price of oats" in Act II is identified with a grain shortage in 1596. Three or four other textual passages substantiate the date.

FIRST EDITION. The play was entered in the "Stationers' Register" in 1598; and a Quarto edition appeared the same year, without any author's name on the title page. In 1599 a Second Quarto appeared, "Newly corrected by W. Shakespeare." Four other Quartos came out successively, in 1604, 1608, 1613, and 1622. Then after the First Folio, of 1623, came two more Quartos, of 1632 and 1639. The texts of all are practically identical.

SOURCES. Holinshed's "Chronicles" and Hall's "Chronicles" are the historical sources of this play, with preference given to the former. There was extant also an old drama entitled "The Famous Victories of Henry V," which had been acted as early as 1598, and which doubtless gave Shakespeare some suggestions. But the earlier play is exceedingly crude in comparison; nor does it yield any comic elements, particularly as to the character of Falstaff, which Shakespeare put to such good use.

ACTION. The historical period extends from June, 1402, to July, 1403, the date of the Battle of Shrewsbury. The dramatic time is about three months, but the actual stage time about ten days.

SELECTED CRITICISM. "With all sorts of readers and spectators this is the greatest favorite of the whole of Shakespeare's English histories, and, indeed, is perhaps the most popular of all dramatic compositions in the language. . . . It is probably owing quite as much to Falstaff and to Hotspur as to the several merits of the other histories . . . that this whole dramatic series of histories . . . have become substituted in the popular mind for all other history of the period. . . . Of the ten plays of this historic series, the *First Part of Henry the Fourth* is the most brilliant and various, and, therefore, the most attractive."—VERPLANCK.

THE SECOND PART OF

KING HENRY THE FOURTH

Present play contains an Induction, an Epilogue, 5 Acts,
19 Scenes, 3099 lines

CAST OF CHARACTERS

RUMOUR, *the Presenter*

KING HENRY *the Fourth of England*

HENRY, *Prince of Wales, afterwards* KING KENRY *the Fifth;*
   THOMAS, *Duke of Clarence;* JOHN, *of Lancaster;* HUMPHREY,
   of Gloster, sons to the King

EARL OF WARWICK, EARL OF WESTMORELAND, EARL OF SURREY, GOWER,
   HARCOURT, BLUNT, *of the King's Party*

Lord Chief Justice of the King's Bench

A Servant of the Chief Justice

EARL OF NORTHUMBERLAND; SCROOP, *Archbishop of York;* LORD
   MOWBRAY; LORD HASTINGS; LORD BARDOLPH; SIR JOHN COLE-
   VILLE, *against the King*

TRAVERS; MORTON, *retainers of Northumberland*

SIR JOHN FALSTAFF   PISTOL

Page to Falstaff   POINS

BARDOLPH   PETO

SHALLOW, SILENCE, *country justices*

DAVY, *servant to Shallow*

MOULDY, SHADOW, WART, FEEBLE, BULLCALF, *recruits*

FANG, SNARE, *sheriff's officers*

LADY NORTHUMBERLAND

LADY PERCY

MISTRESS QUICKLY, *hostess of a tavern in Eastcheap*

DOLL TEARSHEET

Lords, Attendants, Porter, Drawers, Beadles, Grooms, and others

A Dancer, Speaker of the Epilogue

SCENE: *England*

127

ACT I

The Earl of Northumberland receives news of his son Hotspur's defeat and death; also that the King has despatched against him an army under the conduct of his second son, Prince John of Lancaster, and the Earl of Westmoreland. Though in feeble health, he resolves to resist. Meantime the generalship of the insurgent forces devolves upon Scroop, Archbishop of York.

ACT II

Sir John Falstaff, though entrusted with a commission for levying a company of royal troops, cannot neglect his personal interests at the tavern. He runs up an account with the hostess and narrowly escapes being sued for the debt. He is found in the tavern by the Prince of Wales, who has just returned from his victorious engagement at Shrewsbury; and the corpulent knight is summoned to forsake his cups and resume his military duties.

ACT III

Falstaff's recruiting is more successful for his purse than for the army, since he releases able-bodied men who can buy themselves out of service, and retains weak, indifferent fellows who hardly serve for targets.

The King grows despondent on account of failing health and the northern insurrection. He cannot be persuaded but that the rebels will menace his throne; and he bemoans the wars which prevent his crusade to the Holy Land.

ACT IV

The insurgent army under the Archbishop of York faces the royal forces of Prince John in Gaultree Forest, Yorkshire. The latter, instead of hazarding a general engagement, invites the rising chieftains to a conference, in which he promises redress of their alleged grievances, proclaims peace, and urges a dispersion of both armies. The insurgents take him at his word and dismiss their forces; whereupon the perfidious prince, who had previously given secret instructions to his own army to fall upon the scattered insurgent bands, seizes on the persons of York and the other rebel leaders and condemns them to be executed for treason. The news of the discomfiture of the insurgent army is carried to the sick King, who, however, is too feeble to evince much interest in the tidings. He sinks rapidly.

The Prince of Wales is summoned from his tavern circle to attend his father, whom he finds in a stupor, with the crown beside him on the pillow. Believing him to be dead, the Prince removes the crown to another room—and thereby incurs the bitter reproaches of the King, who believes his son desirous of his death. Prince Henry justifies his conduct, and the two are reconciled.

ACT V

Shortly afterwards Henry IV passes away, and the Prince of Wales is crowned Henry V. No sooner does he assume his regal dignities than he dismisses from his society Sir John Falstaff and his convivial crew, and resolves henceforth to prove worthy of his high office.

NOTES

Since the *Second Part of Henry the Fourth* is a close continuation of the *First Part,* both in text and stage presentation, it may be assigned to 1597 or 1598. There is an allusion in Act V to Amurath III whose death occurred early in 1596. Ben Jonson, in 1599, refers to Justice Silence, one of the characters.

FIRST EDITIONS. A Quarto edition was published in 1600, saying, "As it hath been sundry times publicly acted by the right honorable, the Lord Chamberlain his Servants. Written by William Shakespeare." It was entered in the "Stationers' Register" the same year. There were apparently no other Quartos; and the next printing was in the First Folio, of 1623.

SOURCES. The sources for this play were the same as those for the *First Part*. The reader is referred to the Notes for that play.

ACTION. The historic period begins with the Battle of Shrewsbury, in 1403, and extends ten years, or to the coronation of Henry V. The dramatic period occupies about two months. Nine days are represented on the stage.

SELECTED CRITICISM. "The political movements of Henry IV's reign, as told by Shakespeare's standard authorities, Holinshed and Hall offered little salient matter for the dramatist. Nevertheless it is here that he most decisively abandons the boldly reconstructive methods of Marlowe; here that he unfolds with most consummate power his own method of creating character and detail within the limits of a general fidelity to recorded fact. He supplements the chroniclers' tale and interprets their silence with a prodigal magnificence of invention unapproached in the other Histories."—HEREFORD.

THE LIFE OF

KING HENRY THE FIFTH

❧ ❧ ❧

*Present play contains 5 Prologues, 1 Epilogue, 5 Acts, 23
Scenes, 3215 lines*

CAST OF CHARACTERS

KING HENRY *the Fifth, of England*

DUKE OF GLOSTER,
DUKE OF BEDFORD, } *brothers to the King*

DUKE OF EXETER, *uncle to the King*

DUKE OF YORK, *cousin to the King*

EARL OF SALISBURY

EARL OF WARWICK

BISHOP *of Ely*

LORD SCROOP

EARL OF WESTMORELAND

ARCHBISHOP *of Canterbury*

EARL *of Cambridge*

SIR THOMAS GREY

SIR THOMAS ERPINGHAM, GOWER, FLUELLEN, MACMORRIS, JAMY,
officers in King Henry's army

BATES, COURT, WILLIAMS, *soldiers in the same*

PISTOL

NYM

BARDOLPH

BOY

A Herald

CHARLES *the Sixth, King of France*

LEWIS, *the Dauphin*

DUKE OF BURGUNDY

DUKE OF ORLEANS

DUKE OF BOURBON

The Constable of France

131

RAMBURES, ⎫
GRANDPRE, ⎬ *French Lords*

Governor of Harfleur
MONTJOY, *a French Herald*
Ambassadors to the King of England
ISABEL, *Queen of France*
KATHARINE, *daughter to Charles and Isabel*
ALICE, *a Lady attending on Princess Katharine*
Hostess of a Tavern in Eastcheap, formerly Mistress Quickly, and now married to Pistol
Lords, Ladies, Officers, Soldiers, Citizens, Messengers, and Attendants
Chorus

SCENE: *England; France*

ACT I

Soon after his coronation, Henry V resolves to secure his title to the crown and augment his popularity with the masses by the splendours of foreign conquest. Accordingly he lays claim to the throne of France through the medium of the ancient Salic law, and declares war against that country. In answer to his first demands for certain French dukedoms, the Dauphin sends back to him in mockery a bag of tennis-balls—the French heir-apparent believing that he has still to deal with a madcap prince.

ACT II

At this time, however, the young monarch's accession of virtues and regal dignities is a source of marvel and admiration; for he has made good his promise, given upon assuming the crown, to forsake the wild companions of his youth. But Sir John Falstaff cannot fathom the sudden change, and dies of a broken heart.

The King imbues all England with his military enthusiasm. A large army is speedily levied and makes ready to embark at Southampton. The French, growing apprehensive at this warlike display, seek to check the invasion by treacherous means, and bribe three English lords to murder the King at the time of his embarkation. The plot is discovered and the King sentences the traitors to death.

ACT III

King Henry storms the French city of Harfleur, which, lacking support, is forced to capitulate. But sickness and privation now make such inroads upon his army that he finds himself in danger of annihilation at the hands of a French force led by the Dauphin, outnumbering his own five to one. Nevertheless he does not avoid battle but pitches camp near the French at Agincourt.

ACT IV

The French are so confident of victory that they cast dice for the disposal of the contemplated prisoners. On the English side all is watchfulness and preparation. The King in person goes disguised through his camp to learn the temper of his men. At daybreak the armies meet in the shock of battle. The Dauphin's forces suffer a disgraceful and overwhelming defeat through lack of generalship.

ACT V

The French are forced to sue for peace. King Henry's terms include, among other things, the recognition of himself as heir to the throne of France, and the bestowal upon him of the hand of the Princess Katharine. All the terms are agreed to. The English conquerors are received at the court of France amid protestations of amity, while the English king and the French princess arrive at a mutual understanding of hearts despite their ignorance of tongues.

NOTES

Henry the Fifth may be ascribed with some certainty to the year 1599. It logically follows the two parts of *Henry the Fourth*, the dates of which are likewise exact. A mention of Essex's name would show that the play was performed somewhere between March 27 and September 28, 1599. In the Prologue reference is made to the Globe Theater, which was built in 1599.

FIRST EDITIONS. The play was entered in the "Stationers' Register," in 1600—and a Quarto appeared the same year, without Shakespeare's name on the title page. Neither was his authorship mentioned in succeeding Quartos of 1602 and 1608. These Quarto versions are all incomplete and faulty, omitting the Prologues and Epilogue, together with about 500 lines of the text proper. These omissions were supplied by the First Folio, of 1623, which evidently went back to an authentic stage version that may have been left in manuscript form.

SOURCES. Holinshed's "Chronicles" is the chief source of historical data for *Henry the Fifth*, though he constantly departs from it in minor situations for the sake of dramatic effect. The old play, "The Famous Victories of Henry the Fifth," mentioned in connection with the preceding plays, gives the dramatist suggestions for only two or three episodes.

ACTION. The historical period extends from the King's opening of Parliament, in 1414, to Henry's betrothal of Katharine, in 1420. The stage time represented is about ten days.

SELECTED CRITICISM. "In order to preserve continuity of style with the foregoing plays, Shakespeare has interspersed *Henry V* with comic figures and scenes. Falstaff himself does not appear, his death being announced at the beginning of the play; but the members of his gang wander around, as living and ludicrous mementoes of him, until they disappear one by one by way of the gallows, so that nothing may survive to recall the great king's frivolous youth."—BRANDES.

KING HENRY THE SIXTH

Present play contains 5 Acts, 27 Scenes, 2665 lines

CAST OF CHARACTERS

KING HENRY *the Sixth, of England*

DUKE OF GLOUCESTER, *uncle to the King, and Protector*

DUKE OF BEDFORD, *uncle to the King, and Regent of France*

THOMAS BEAUFORT, *Duke of Exeter, great-uncle to the King*

HENRY BEAUFORT, *great-uncle to the King, Bishop of Winchester and afterwards Cardinal*

JOHN BEAUFORT, *Earl, afterwards Duke, of Somerset*

RICHARD PLANTAGENET, *son to Richard, late Earl of Cambridge, afterwards Duke of York*

EARL OF WARWICK

EARL OF SALISBURY

EARL OF SUFFOLK

LORD TALBOT, *afterwards Earl of Shrewsbury*

JOHN TALBOT, *son to Lord Talbot*

EDMUND MORTIMER, *Earl of March*

SIR JOHN FASTOLFE

SIR WILLIAM LUCY

SIR WILLIAM GLANSDALE

SIR THOMAS GARGRAVE

MAYOR *of London*

WOODVILLE, *Lieutenant of the Tower*

VERNON, *of the White Rose or York faction*

BASSET, *of the Red Rose or Lancaster faction*

A Lawyer

Mortimer's Keepers

CHARLES, *Dauphin, and afterwards King of France*

REIGNIER, *Duke of Anjou; titular King of Naples*

DUKE OF BURGUNDY

DUKE OF ALENÇON

BASTARD OF ORLEANS

Governor of Paris

MASTER-GUNNER *of Orleans, and his Son*

General of the French forces in Bordeaux

A French Sergeant

A Porter

An old Shepherd, father to Joan la Pucelle

MARGARET, *daughter to Reignier, afterwards married to King Henry*

COUNTESS OF AUVERGNE

JOAN LA PUCELLE, *commonly called Joan of Arc*

Fiends appearing to La Pucelle

Lords, Warders of the Tower, Heralds, Officers, Soldiers, Messengers, and Attendants

SCENE: *England; France*

ACT I

The martial Henry V, conqueror of France, dies in the culmination of his glory, leaving to his son, Henry VI, the two sceptres of England and France. But the young monarch, still in his minority, is surrounded by warring nobles who lose sight of their country's foreign interests in private broils. They fail to send their general, Lord Talbot, adequate forces for his French campaign.

The French seize upon this moment of English weakness to retake many of their cities and the Dauphin receives unexpected aid from a shepherd's daughter, Joan la Pucelle, better known as Joan of Arc, who first assists him to raise the siege of Orleans, notwithstanding the valiant resistance of Talbot.

ACT II

While the French celebrate their victory with feasting in Orleans, the English plan an attack, and by a sudden night sortie retake Orleans.

In England, meanwhile, the violent feuds of Richard Plantagenet, afterwards Duke of York, and John Beaufort, Earl, afterwards Duke of Somerset, whose parties are distinguished by white and red roses, develop into civil strife which was ere long to deluge the entire kingdom with blood.

ACT III

The French, through the strategy of Joan of Arc, capture Rouen; but Talbot's forces in a desperate charge retake the city. An English garrison is placed on the walls, and Talbot proceeds with his army to Paris, whither the young King Henry VI has come for his second coronation. The King recognises the merit of his general by creating Talbot Earl of Shrewsbury. The French Duke of Burgundy, who had been serving in conjunction with the English army, and had set out from Rouen a little behind Talbot, is met by the Dauphin and persuaded to turn his allegiance to France.

ACT IV

The intrepid Talbot and his son attempt to take Bordeaux, but are entrapped by a greatly superior force under the Dauphin. The personal quarrels of York and Somerset cause them to deny reinforcements promised to Talbot, and he is slain in a bloody battle.

ACT V

The French on their side suffer a loss in the capture of Joan of Arc, who is cruelly condemned to death at the stake for witchcraft. The war brings varying fortunes to both sides, until at last overtures of peace are made. The Dauphin consents to swear allegiance to England and reign as viceroy, while King Henry is induced by the artful suggestions of the Earl of Suffolk to forego a proposed matrimonial alliance with the daughter of the Earl of Armagnac, and to solicit the hand of Margaret, daughter of the Duke of Anjou.

NOTES

There seems to be little doubt that the *First Part of Henry the Sixth* is one of the earliest of the Shakespearean plays; there was, however, considerable doubt as to Shakespeare's own part in the first text. The play was definitely referred to by Nash, in 1592, and by Henslowe in 1591. In 1592 Greene, a fellow playwright, made a satirical attack upon Shakespeare, which also serves to link the latter up with the *Third Part* of this play. Other textual evidence places the *First Part* somewhere between 1589 and 1591.

FIRST EDITION.   The earliest edition extant is that of the First Folio, of 1623, and it is mentioned in the "Register" of that year as "not formerly entered to other men." There can be little doubt that the first texts mentioned above were not by Shakespeare; and that he worked over or in collaboration with others upon this play.

SOURCES.   Holinshed's "Chronicles" and Hall's "Chronicle" are the historical sources of all three parts of *Henry the Sixth*. Holinshed, however, is not followed so closely as in later historical plays.

ACTION.   *Part First* deals with the historical period from the death of Henry V, 1422, to the marriage agreement between Henry VI and Margaret, in 1444. The stage time is about eight days.

SELECTED CRITICISM.   "Shakespeare's choice fell first on this period of English history, so full of misery and horrors of every kind, because the pathetic is naturally more suitable than the characteristic to a young poet's mind. We do not yet find here the whole maturity of his genius, yet certainly its whole strength. Careless as to the apparent unconnectedness of contemporary events, he bestows little attention on preparation and development; all the figures follow in rapid succession, and announce themselves emphatically for what we ought to take them."—SCHLEGEL.

KING HENRY THE SIXTH

Present play contains 5 Acts, 24 Scenes, 3094 lines

CAST OF CHARACTERS

KING HENRY *the Sixth, of England*

HUMPHREY, *Duke of Gloucester, uncle to the King*

CARDINAL BEAUFORT, *Bishop of Winchester, great-uncle to the King*

RICHARD PLANTAGENET, *Duke of York*

EDWARD, RICHARD, *sons to York*

DUKE OF SOMERSET

DUKE OF SUFFOLK

DUKE OF BUCKINGHAM

LORD CLIFFORD

Young CLIFFORD, *son to Clifford*

EARL OF SALISBURY

EARL OF WARWICK

LORD SCALES

LORD SAY

SIR HUMPHREY STAFFORD

WILLIAM STAFFORD, *brother to Sir Humphrey*

SIR JOHN STANLEY

VAUX

MATTHEW GOFFE

WALTER WHITMORE

A Sea-captain

A Master

A Master's-mate

Two Gentlemen, prisoners with Suffolk

JOHN HUME, JOHN SOUTHWELL, *priests*

ROGER BOLINGBROKE, *a conjurer*

THOMAS HORNER, *an armorer*

PETER, *servant to armorer*
Clerk of Chatham
Mayor of Saint Alban's
SIMPCOX, *an impostor*
ALEXANDER IDEN, *a Kentish gentleman*
JACK CADE, *a rebel*
GEORGE BEVIS, JOHN HOLLAND, DICK, *the butcher,* SMITH, *the weaver*
MICHAEL, *Two Murderers, followers of Cade*
MARGARET, *Queen to King Henry*
ELEANOR, *Duchess of Gloucester*
MARGARET JOURDAIN, *a witch*
Wife to Simpcox
*Lords, Ladies, Attendants, Petitioners, Aldermen, Herald,
    Beadle, Sheriff, Officers, Citizens, 'Prentices, Falconers,
    Guards, Soldiers, Messengers*
A Spirit

SCENE: *England*

ACT I

Margaret of Anjou is brought over to England and wedded to
King Henry VI; but—much to the consternation of the King's
uncle, Gloucester, the lord protector—she comes dowerless, and
the duchies for which Henry V warred are suffered to remain
in French hands. Though the upright Gloucester's grief is
strongly uttered, he is not upheld when he unburdens it to the
other nobles. Instead, they make a temporary truce of their own
quarrelling, which has proceeded continuously during the young
King's reign, and unite against the lord protector. They find a
ready ally in the Queen, who is eager to secure unlimited con-
trol over her weak husband. They make their first attack through
Gloucester's ambitious wife. She is betrayed into harbouring
sorcerers who raise up a spirit that utters sayings against the
heads of the realm. She and the conjurers are taken into custody.

ACT II

The Duchess of Gloucester is brought to trial and banished.
Gloucester is deprived of his post of lord protector, and is summoned before Parliament.

Meanwhile the strife between the houses of York and Lancaster gathers force. The Duke of York convinces the powerful earls of Warwick and Salisbury of his right to the crown.

ACT III

Gloucester answers the summons and appears before Parliament. He is accused of high treason and committed to prison, and since his accusers can find no evidence to support their charge against his integrity, he is foully assassinated by direction of the Duke of Suffolk. The populace, learning of the deed, are driven to desperation, and storm the palace, demanding the death or exile of Suffolk, who is forthwith banished, and afterwards is slain at sea by pirates.

The powerless monarch's sway is marked by continued losses. News comes of the loss of the last of the French territories. Other tidings tell of an uprising in Ireland. The lords, jealous of York's power, think to be rid of him by sending him against the Irish. York, however, is glad of the pretext to muster an army; and before he sets sail he incites a rebellion at home under Jack Cade, a Kentish labourer.

ACT IV

After meeting with one or two small successes, seizing London Bridge, and entering the city, Cade's forces are dispersed by the royal troops. The populace renew allegiance to the King, and sue for pardon, which is granted. But a price is placed on the head of the fugitive Cade, and he is slain. York's connexion with this rebellion has been hidden; but upon hearing of its outcome he returns to England at the head of his army, ostensibly to redress private wrongs, though really to assist his claim to the throne.

ACT V

The King holds parley with York near Blackheath, but the conference ends in open defiance on the part of the subject. The two armies meet in conflict on the field of St. Albans, where

the King, who now represents the Lancastrians, is defeated and
forced to fly towards London. The victorious York and Warwick
resolve to march rapidly upon the capital.

NOTES

The *Second Part of Henry the Sixth* evidently followed the *First
Part* very closely both in composition and acting. We have already
noted, in the preceding play, that its date was between 1589 and
1591. Greene's attack upon Shakespeare, in 1592, referred particularly to the *Third Part*. The *Second Part* may therefore be safely
assigned to 1591.

FIRST EDITIONS.   Unlike the earlier play, the *Second Part* has come
down to us in Quarto form, dated 1594, but anonymously and with
this title: "The First Part of the contention betwixt the two famous
houses of York and Lancaster," etc. A second Quarto with the same
text and title appeared in 1600; and a third in 1619—the latter
being the earliest to include Shakespeare's name as the author. The
First Folio, of 1623, shows many important variations from the
Quarto text.

SOURCES.   Holinshed's "Chronicles" and Hall's "Chronicle" are the
sources of all the *Henry the Sixth* plays.

ACTION.   The historic period covers about ten years, from the
Queen's crowning, in 1445, to the Battle of St. Albans, in 1455. The
stage action is about fourteen days.

SELECTED CRITICISM.   *"The Second Part of Henry the Sixth* is
manifestly a great advance upon the *First,* and that in nearly all the
particulars of dramatic excellence. The several members are well
knit together; the characterization is bold, but in the main firm and
steady; the action clear, free, and generally carried on in that con-
secutiveness that every later part seems the natural growth and issue
of what had gone before. Much of this superiority, no doubt, was
owing to the nature of the materials, which, besides yielding a
greater variety of interest, were of themselves more limber and
pliant to the shaping of art, and presented less to distract and baffle
the powers of dramatic assortment and composition."—HUDSON.

KING HENRY THE SIXTH

❧ ❧ ❧

Present play contains 5 Acts, 28 Scenes, 2896 lines

CAST OF CHARACTERS

KING HENRY *the Sixth, of England*

EDWARD, *Prince of Wales*

LEWIS *the Eleventh, King of France*

DUKE OF SOMERSET

DUKE OF EXETER

EARL OF OXFORD

EARL OF NORTHUMBERLAND

EARL OF WESTMORELAND

LORD CLIFFORD

RICHARD PLANTAGENET, *Duke of York*

EDWARD, *Earl of March, afterwards King Edward the Fourth;* EDMUND, *Earl of Rutland;* GEORGE, *afterwards Duke of Clarence;* RICHARD, *afterwards Duke of Gloucester, sons to York*

DUKE OF NORFOLK

MARQUESS OF MONTAGUE

EARL OF WARWICK

EARL OF PEMBROKE

LORD HASTINGS

LORD STAFFORD

SIR JOHN MORTIMER, SIR HUGH MORTIMER, *uncles to the Duke of York*

HENRY, *Earl of Richmond, a youth*

LORD RIVERS, *brother to Lady Grey*

SIR WILLIAM STANLEY

SIR JOHN MONTGOMERY

SIR JOHN SOMERVILLE

Tutor to Rutland

Mayor of York
Lieutenant of the Tower
A Nobleman
Two Keepers
A Huntsman
A Son that has killed his father
A Father that has killed his son
MARGARET, *Queen to King Henry*
LADY ELIZABETH GREY, *afterwards Queen to Edward the Fourth*
BONA, *sister to the French Queen*
Soldiers, Attendants, Messengers, Watchmen, and others
SCENE: *England; France*

ACT I

The Duke of York reaches London in advance of the King, and is seated by Warwick upon the throne. There the weak-kneed monarch shortly afterwards finds him; nor can he move him from his seat till York is promised the kingly succession after Henry's death. Neither of the rival houses long abides by the treaty. The haughty Queen Margaret becomes enraged at the prospect of her son's deposition, and herself musters an army against York, who is defeated and slain.

ACT II

York's sons, Edward and Richard, though much depressed by these tidings, take heart again upon being joined by the powerful Warwick. The royal forces are engaged once more near Towton. The battle is fiercely fought, but at length the King's— or, more properly, the Queen's—forces are routed. Edward proceeds to London to mount the throne as Edward IV.

ACT III

Having witnessed Edward's coronation, Warwick crosses over to France to obtain for the new sovereign the hand of the Princess Bona. At the French court he encounters Queen Margaret and her son, who had come to implore the French King's aid in their cause. This is almost granted when the arrival of Warwick changes the aspect of affairs, and Edward's overtures are successful. Just at this moment, however, letters from England bear intelligence that Edward has married Lady Elizabeth Grey. Naturally both the King of France and Warwick are incensed at the broken faith. Warwick then and there becomes reconciled with Queen Margaret, who is also promised French forces to renew the struggle.

ACT IV

Warwick hurries back to England, surprises Edward by forced marches, takes the crown from his head, and gives it back to Henry, who has been languishing in the Tower. But Edward in turn escapes from Warwick's surveillance, and takes refuge in Burgundy, where he recruits fresh troops. Upon returning to England he proceeds to his dukedom of York, and soon gathers strength enough to march on London. The impotent Henry is again seized and consigned to the Tower.

ACT V

Edward meets Warwick in an engagement near Barnet, and the great earl, whose deeds have given him the title of "King-maker," is slain. A still more decisive battle is fought and won against Queen Margaret and the remnants of the Lancastrian forces, supported by the French, on the plains of Tewksbury. Queen Margaret is taken prisoner, and her son is stabbed to the heart by the three brothers of York. Henry's weak, troubled reign is ended by a dagger-thrust at the hands of Edward's brother, Richard of Gloucester; while Edward assumes the crown so bloodily striven for, amid every prospect of peace for himself and security for his infant son. Destiny has not yet revealed the sinister intentions of the ambitious Gloucester.

NOTES

In 1592, a fellow actor, Robert Greene, accused Shakespeare of plagiarism. His attack referred more particularly to the *Third Part of Henry the Sixth;* and it is evident, therefore, that this play appeared in 1591 or 1592. Textual evidence supports this date, but is not reliable, as all the early texts of the three plays dealing with Henry the Sixth are faulty and show traces of several authors.

FIRST EDITIONS. This play first appeared in Quarto form, in 1595, without Shakespeare's name, the title being: "The True Tragedy of Richard Duke of Yorke, and the Death of good King Henry the Sixth," etc. A Second Quarto, following the same version, appeared in 1600. In 1619, the Third Quarto appeared, with Shakespeare's name on the title page, and in conjunction with "The Contention," etc., which was later the *Second Part.* It remained for the First Folio, of 1623, to disentangle texts and titles and arrange them as three parts of one play.

SOURCES. Holinshed's "Chronicles" and Hall's "Chronicle" are the historical sources of all three parts of this play.

ACTION. The action historically closely follows the preceding play —beginning with the Battle of St. Albans, 1455, and closing with Henry's death, in 1471. The stage time is about twenty days.

SELECTED CRITICISM. "Let us take a survey of the whole trilogy. . . . We have history represented in its degeneration into civil war, which is the consequence of the original disturbance of its course and of the general demoralization which increases with it. This is the theme upon which the whole trilogy is based, and which exhibits the two sides of life according to Shakespeare's conception. . . . History punishes every uncalled-for interference as unauthorized presumption, whereas the submissive spirit is inwardly exalted and glorified through suffering and death. This is the thought which connects the events of the *Third Part* into an organic unity."—ULRICI.

KING RICHARD THE THIRD

cᶳ⁰ cᶳ⁰ cᶳ⁰

Present play contains 5 Acts, 25 Scenes, 3578 lines

CAST OF CHARACTERS

KING EDWARD *the Fourth, of England*

EDWARD, *Prince of Wales, afterwards King Edward the Fifth;*
    RICHARD, *Duke of York, sons to the King*

GEORGE, *Duke of Clarence;* RICHARD, *Duke of Gloucester, after-*
    wards King Richard the Third, brothers to the King

A young son of Clarence

HENRY, *Earl of Richmond, afterwards King Henry the Seventh*

CARDINAL BOURCHIER, *Archbishop of Canterbury*

THOMAS ROTHERHAM, *Archbishop of York*

JOHN MORTON, *Bishop of Ely*

DUKE OF BUCKINGHAM

DUKE OF NORFOLK

EARL OF SURREY, *son to Norfolk*

EARL RIVERS, *brother to Queen Elizabeth*

MARQUIS OF DORSET, LORD GREY, *sons to Queen Elizabeth*

EARL OF OXFORD

LORD STANLEY, *also called* EARL OF DERBY

LORD HASTINGS

LORD LOVEL

SIR THOMAS VAUGHN

SIR RICHARD RATCLIFF

SIR WALTER HERBERT

SIR WILLIAM CATESBY

SIR JAMES TYRREL

SIR JAMES BLOUNT

SIR ROBERT BRACKENBURY, *Lieutenant of the Tower*

CHRISTOPHER URSWICK, *a priest*

Another Priest

TRESSEL *and* BERKELEY, *gentlemen attending on the Lady Anne*
Lord Mayor of London
Sheriff of Wiltshire
ELIZABETH, *Queen to King Edward the Fourth*
MARGARET, *widow of King Henry the Sixth*
DUCHESS OF YORK, *mother to King Edward the Fourth*
LADY ANNE, *widow of Edward, Prince of Wales, son to King*
    Henry the Sixth; afterwards married to Richard of Glouces-
    ter
A young daughter of Clarence (MARGARET PLANTAGENET)
Ghosts of those murdered by Richard the Third
Lords, Attendants, Pursuivant, Scrivener, Citizens, Murderers,
    Messengers, Soldiers, and others
                    SCENE: *England*

ACT I

Richard, Duke of Gloucester, resolves to obtain the crown of
England, notwithstanding the fact that he is not in the direct
line of succession. He aims a secret blow against his brother
Clarence, who is involved by him in a quarrel with their
brother, King Edward IV, and immured in the Tower, where
he is shortly afterwards murdered. Gloucester next seeks to
strengthen his cause by suing for the hand of Lady Anne, which
he wins in the very presence of the corpse of her father-in-law,
Henry VI, dead at his hands, and despite the fact that her
husband had also been slain by him.

ACT II

King Edward, in declining health, seeks to foster peace in his
realm. He dies, and his young son Edward, Prince of Wales,
is summoned to London to be crowned. Before he arrives,
Gloucester, who is made lord protector, finds means to weaken
the prince by imprisoning and afterwards executing three noblemen of the latter's party.

ACT III

Richard meets the prince and his younger brother in London, and under pretext of assigning them a lodging imprisons them in the Tower. Lord Hastings, a powerful nobleman faithful to the royal line, is beheaded, also by Richard's orders. The Duke of Buckingham upholds Gloucester, and is largely instrumental in obtaining for him the coveted crown.

ACT IV

Buckingham, however, hesitates when the new King Richard III desires at his hands the lives of the two princes; and he is further disaffected by the King's refusal to grant him a certain earldom previously promised as a reward for his support. He accordingly forsakes Richard and seeks to unite his strength with that of Henry, Earl of Richmond, who is taking up arms against the usurping monarch. Buckingham is taken prisoner and soon afterwards put to death. The two boy princes are assassinated in the Tower; and Queen Anne is secretly put to death in order to leave Richard free for an alliance with the heiress of York, Elizabeth, daughter of Edward IV, for whose hand he sues to her mother.

ACT V

In the meantime Richmond has invaded England and encounters Richard's forces at Bosworth Field in Leicestershire. The King, though disquieted on the preceding night by visions of his many slain victims, fights desperately; but his forces are defeated and he himself is slain by Richmond. The victor is recognized as King Henry VII, and by marriage with Elizabeth of York brings to a close the long contention between the rival houses of York and Lancaster.

NOTES

Richard the Third was certainly written before 1597, the date of its first printing. John Weever, in his "Epigrams," written in 1595, mentions "Richard," and this play seems intended. Other textual evidence places the play about 1594.

FIRST EDITIONS.   In 1597 a Quarto edition appeared, with a lengthy title, but no mention of Shakespeare's name. A Second Quarto came out the next year, with the same title, but different publisher, and with "William Shakespeare," as author. The Third Quarto, 1602, stated that it was "Newly augmented by William Shakespeare." Five other Quartos appeared, respectively, in 1605, 1612, 1622, 1629, and 1634. The text of all was substantially the same. The First Folio, of 1623, differs in many respects from the Quartos.

SOURCES.   In 1513, Sir Thomas More wrote a "History of King Richard the Third," which was almost contemporary with its subject. His story was continued by Grafton. Holinshed and Hall, in their "Chronicles," are clearly indebted to More. While Shakespeare may have seen the earlier material he bases his text on Holinshed. Another play on the same subject by an unknown author (1594) bears little if any resemblance to Shakespeare's.

ACTION.   This play is a close continuation of the *Third Part of Henry the Sixth,* beginning with that monarch's death, in 1471, and ending with the Battle of Bosworth Field, in 1485. The stage time is eleven days.

SELECTED CRITICISM.   "Certain qualities which make it unique among the dramas of Shakespeare characterize the play of *Richard the Third*. Its manner of conceiving and presenting character has a certain resemblance, not elsewhere to be found in Shakespeare's writings, to the ideal manner of Marlowe. As in the plays of Marlowe, there is here one dominant figure distinguished by a few strongly marked and inordinately developed qualities. There is in the characterization no mystery, but much of demoniac intensity."
   —DOWDEN.

KING HENRY THE EIGHTH

❧ ❧ ❧

*Present play contains Prologue, Epilogue, 5 Acts, 16 Scenes,
2809 lines*

CAST OF CHARACTERS

KING HENRY *the Eighth, of England*
CARDINAL WOLSEY
CARDINAL CAMPEIUS
CAPUCIUS, *Ambassador from the Emperor Charles the Fifth*
CRANMER, *Archbishop of Canterbury*
DUKE OF NORFOLK
DUKE OF BUCKINGHAM
DUKE OF SUFFOLK
EARL OF SURREY
LORD CHAMBERLAIN
LORD CHANCELLOR
GARDINER, *Bishop of Winchester*
Bishop of Lincoln
LORD ABERGAVENNY
LORD SANDS
SIR HENRY GUILDFORD
SIR THOMAS LOVELL
SIR ANTHONY DENNY
SIR NICHOLAS VAUX
Secretaries to Wolsey
CROMWELL, *servant to Wolsey*
GRIFFITH, *gentleman-usher to Queen Katharine*
Three gentlemen
DOCTOR BUTTS, *physician to the King*
Garter King-at-arms
Surveyor to the Duke of Buckingham

BRANDON
Sergeant-at-arms
Doorkeeper of the Council-chamber
Porter, and his Man
Page to Gardiner
A Crier
QUEEN KATHARINE, *wife to King Henry, afterwards divorced*
ANNE BULLEN, *her Maid of Honour, afterwards Queen*
An old Lady, friend to Anne Bullen
PATIENCE, *woman to Queen Katharine*
Several Lords and Ladies in the Dumb Shows; Women attend-
ing upon the Queen; Scribes, Officers, Guards, and other
Attendants
Spirits

SCENE: *London, Westminster; Kimbolton*

ACT I

Soon after the return of the English court from the Field of the Cloth of Gold, the Duke of Buckingham has the misfortune to embroil himself with Cardinal Wolsey, chancellor to Henry VIII. The cardinal suborns some discontented servants of the duke to accuse their master of treasonable purposes, Wolsey's desire to work Buckingham's downfall probably being strengthened by jealousy of his power.

Wolsey gives a great supper to the court, which is attended by the King and his lords masked. Henry is greatly attracted by the beauty of Anne Bullen, a maid of honour.

ACT II

Buckingham is brought to trial, convicted of high treason and led to execution.

The charms of Anne Bullen awaken in the King a long dormant scruple of conscience regarding the legality of his marriage with Katharine, the widow of his deceased brother. He resolves to divorce the Queen, and calls her to public trial. She attends, but refuses to submit to the court. She will not accept Wolsey for judge, and appeals to the Pope.

ACT III

The cardinal, now seeing the drift of Henry's purpose, and dismayed at the prospect of his union with a Protestant, takes the side of Queen Katharine and sends private instructions to the papal court that her divorce may be delayed. But the Queen still mistrusts him for her enemy. The King, meanwhile becoming impatient at Rome's delay, takes matters into his own hands, puts away Queen Katharine, and secretly espouses Anne Bullen. At this juncture he by chance gains possession of the cardinal's papers—the letter to the Pope, and an inventory of the chancellor's enormous wealth. The enraged monarch deprives Wolsey of his civil offices, and the fallen favourite is saved from a charge of high treason only by the interposition of death.

ACT IV

The divorced Queen Katharine shortly follows Wolsey to the grave. Anne Bullen is publicly crowned as Queen amid much ceremony, being anointed by Cranmer, Archbishop of Canterbury.

ACT V

After Wolsey's death Cranmer enjoys a great share of the King's favour. This arouses the jealousy of powerful nobles, who form a conspiracy against the prelate. He is brought to trial and threatened with imprisonment in the Tower, when the opportune arrival of Henry himself enables him to triumph over his rivals. Cranmer evinces his gratitude for the royal friendship by taking part in the christening of Queen Anne's infant daughter, Elizabeth, for whom he prophesies a career of great splendour.

NOTES

The Globe Theater burned down, in 1613, during a performance of *Henry the Eighth* which was noted as "a new play." Three or four allusions to this catastrophe identify the play with Shakespeare's. Other textual evidence place it in 1612 or 1613.

FIRST EDITION. The earliest text now known is the First Folio, of 1623. It is unusually free from errors, and as there are no Quarto versions the text has not undergone change of any moment.

SOURCES. Several sources of Shakespeare's material, other than the "Chronicles" of Holinshed and Hall, are indicated; among them, two plays dealing with Cardinal Wolsey, current about 1600. Fox's "Book of Marytrs" (1563) contains suggestions for the Fifth Act. A "Life of Cardinal Wolsey," by one of his retainers, George Cavendish, was an indirect source, as the historians above referred to evidently drew upon it. This play is now believed to be of dual authorship, John Fletcher being the other playwright involved.

ACTION. The historical action covers twenty-four years, from the Field of the Cloth of Gold, 1520, to the trial of Cranmer, 1544. The chronology of the play, however, is not always accurate. The stage time is one week.

SELECTED CRITICISM. "No doubt the nature of the subject imposed enormous difficulties on an Elizabethan dramatist. To render with imaginative sympathy the moving story of the divorce, and yet to remember that the glory of his own time had flowered from that malign plant, was to be under a continual provocation to the conflict of interests which the play, as we see, has not escaped. Regarded near by, the divorce of Katharine was a pitiful tragedy; regarded in retrospect it seemed big with the destinies of England. . . . After making all allowance for such obstacles, it remains true that the total effect of the drama is insignificant in proportion to the splendor of detail and the superb power of single scenes. Nothing more damning can be said of any play, and nothing like it can be said of any play which is wholly Shakespeare's work. Hence, in point simply of dramatic quality the play justifies a suspicion that it is not entirely Shakespeare's work."—HEREFORD.

TROILUS AND CRESSIDA

ꙮ ꙮ ꙮ

Present play contains Prologue, 5 Acts, 25 Scenes, 3342 lines

CAST OF CHARACTERS

PRIAM, *King of Troy*

HECTOR,
TROILUS,
PARIS, } *sons to Priam*
DEIPHOBUS,
HELENUS,

MARGARELON, *a natural son to Priam*

ÆNEAS, } *Trojan commanders*
ANTENOR,

CALCHAS, *a Trojan priest, taking part with the Greeks*

PANDARUS, *uncle to Cressida*

AGAMEMNON, *the Grecian general*

MENELAUS, *his brother*

ACHILLES,
AJAX,
ULYSSES, } *Grecian commanders*
NESTOR,
DIOMEDES,
PATROCLUS,

THERSITES, *a deformed and scurrilous Grecian*

ALEXANDER, *servant to Cressida*   *Servant to Troilus*

Servant to Paris   *Servant to Diomedes*

HELEN, *wife to Menelaus*

ANDROMACHE, *wife to Hector*

CASSANDRA, *daughter to Priam, a prophetess*

CRESSIDA, *daughter to Calchas*

Trojan and Greek Soldiers, and Attendants

SCENE: *Troy, and the Grecian camp before it*

155

ACT I

In the eighth year of the siege of Troy by the Greeks, Troilus, son of King Priam of Troy, becomes enamoured of Cressida, a Trojan maiden, and induces her uncle Pandarus to intercede for him. At this time a truce has been declared between the two armies. While the Greeks are carping at the slowness of the siege, a challenge is sent them by Hector of Troy, directed against any one of their champions who dares meet him in single combat; his evident desire being to cope with Achilles, the Greeks' chief warrior.

ACT II

During the truce the Greeks had proposed terms of peace, which included the return of the ravished Helen and the payment of a war indemnity. The terms are rejected and the besieging generals prepare to renew the struggle. They seek an interview with Achilles, who has for some time sulked within his tent. He denies them an interview, whereupon they select Ajax to fight with Hector.

ACT III

In the interim Pandarus prospers as go-between for Troilus with Cressida. He arranges a rendezvous where the lovers plight their troth and, according to custom, resolve to live together. But Cressida's father, who has been traitorously serving the Greeks, requests them to ask his daughter in exchange for a Trojan leader held captive by them.

ACT IV

The Greeks consent, and send Diomedes to effect the exchange. He bears away Cressida on the morning following her nuptial night. The lovers bewail this stern necessity of war, and part after many protestations of fidelity. Diomedes and Cressida reach the Grecian camp just as Ajax is starting forth to meet Hector. The two warriors fight, but after a passage at arms postpone further conflict on account of kinship. The various Grecian and Trojan leaders make use of this armistice for an interchange of amicable courtesies.

ACT V

Troilus asks the Greek Ulysses to lead him to the tent where Cressida has been confined; and there he is deeply mortified to become a secret witness of her faithlessness, for she has transferred her affections to Diomedes. In battle on the following day, Troilus engages in conflict with Diomedes, but without serious result for either. Meanwhile Hector also has gone forth to battle again, disregarding the ominous predictions of his sister Cassandra. He kills Patroclus, a close friend of Achilles, which deed so enrages that moody warrior, that he shakes off his lethargy, plunges into the fray, and slays Hector, whose dead body he drags at his horse's heels along the field before Troy.

NOTES

It is difficult to assign a definite date to *Troilus and Cressida*. A Quarto version appeared in 1609, but textual changes would indicate a date at least ten years earlier, as the time when the play was written. It seems to have been revised from an earlier version, perhaps by another hand. The "Stationers' Register" contains an entry in 1603 of the book, "as it is acted by my Lord Chamberlain's men"— a company to which Shakespeare belonged.

FIRST EDITIONS. Two Quarto editions appeared in 1609, both having Shakespeare's name on the title page, and the two being identical. The First Folio, of 1623, was the next edition, and shows some minor variations from the earlier version.

SOURCES. The chief sources of this play are: (1) Chaucer's poem, "Troilus and Creseide," which furnishes an idea for the love theme; (2) Caxton's "Recuyell of the Historyes of Troy," and (3) Chapman's translation of Homer's "Iliad," which appeared in part in 1597.

ACTION. Four days comprise the acting time of the play, with allowance for certain intervals. The historical period deals with incidents of the siege of Troy by the Greeks, which extended from 1193 B. C. to 1184 B. C.

SELECTED CRITICISM. "This is the most difficult of all Shakespeare's plays to deal with, as well for date as position. . . . The play is evidently written in ill-humor with mankind; it is a bitter satire. Its purpose is not to show virtue her own feature, but contemptible weakness, paltry vanity, falsehood (like scorn), their own image. . . . Shakespeare's treatment of Chaucer's heroine, Cressida, is, too, a shock to any lover of the early poet's work. . . . There is no relief to the patchery, the jugglery, and the knavery, except the generous welcome of Nestor to Hector in the Grecian camp, and his frank praise of the gallant Trojan, who, laboring for destiny, made cruel way through ranks of Greekish youth."—FURNIVAL.

TITUS ANDRONICUS

⚜ ⚜ ⚜

Present play contains 5 Acts, 16 Scenes, 2514 lines

CAST OF CHARACTERS

SATURNINUS, *son to the late Emperor of Rome, and afterwards declared Emperor*

BASSIANUS, *brother to Saturninus, in love with Lavinia*

TITUS ANDRONICUS, *a noble Roman, general against the Goths*

MARCUS ANDRONICUS, *tribune of the people, and brother to Titus Andronicus*

LUCIUS,
QUINTUS, } *sons to Titus Andronicus*
MARTIUS,
MUTIUS,

YOUNG LUCIUS, *a boy, son to Lucius*

PUBLIUS, *son to Marcus the Tribune*

SEMPRONIUS,
CAIUS, } *kinsmen to Titus*
VALENTINE,

ÆMILIUS, *a noble Roman*

ALARBUS,
DEMETRIUS, } *sons to Tamora*
CHIRON,

AARON, *a Moor, beloved by Tamora*

TAMORA, *Queen of the Goths*

LAVINIA, *daughter to Titus Andronicus*

A Nurse

Captain, Tribune, Messenger, and Clown

Goths and Romans

Senators, Tribunes, Officers, Soldiers, and Attendants

SCENE: *Rome, and its environs*

ACT I

Titus Andronicus, a Roman general, returns home in triumph after a conquest of the Goths, and is hailed by a large part of the people as their next emperor. The inheritance of the crown is just then in controversy between the deceased ruler's two sons. Titus will not take advantage of the dispute and his own popularity, but magnanimously sides with the elder son, Saturninus, who is enabled by this influence to ascend the throne. The new Emperor asks Titus's daughter Lavinia in marriage, which request is granted. But the project is thwarted by the Emperor's younger brother, Bassianus, who carries off Lavinia—to whom he is betrothed—by force. Titus is so enraged at this and so earnest in his faith with Saturninus, that he kills one of his own sons who has aided Bassianus. Nevertheless, the Emperor uses this as a pretext for slighting Titus, whose power he fears; and although he makes quick choice of another wife in the person of Tamora, Queen of the Goths, brought captive by Titus, he seeks the downfall of the general. He finds a ready second in Tamora, who hates Titus because he has offered up her son as a sacrifice to the slain members of his family.

ACT II

Though this deadly hatred exists on the part of the imperial couple, they yet veil it under a show of amity. The deluded Titus seeks to do them honour by giving a hunt, which ends as a chapter of horrors. The Empress seizes the opportunity to meet her lover, a cruel and crafty Moor named Aaron. By a series of devilish plots he incites Tamora's two sons to ravish Lavinia, tear out her tongue, and cut off her hands, so that she cannot denounce them either in speech or writing. Bassianus is slain, and the Moor directs suspicion against two sons of Titus.

ACT III

The two sons are sentenced and led to execution. Aaron gives Titus to understand that their lives will be spared if he will cut off his hand and send it to the Emperor. Titus complies, but is mocked by the Moor, who returns the hand with the heads of the two sons. Henceforth Titus devotes his whole life to vengeance.

ACT IV

Pretending madness he sends strange messages to the Emperor, and also to Tamora's sons, whom he discovers to be the authors of Lavinia's shame.

Meantime another son of Titus, named Lucius, being banished from Rome, gathers together a powerful army of Goths, who menace the city. Tamora finds it necessary to hold a parley with him at his father's house.

ACT V

To arrange the interview, she goes with her two sons disguised, to Titus's house. He still feigns insanity and, after she departs, kills the sons and bakes their remains in a pie. The pie is shortly after offered to Tamora at a feast, when she and the Emperor meet Lucius in parley. It is a fitting dish for a bloody banquet, since, at the general slaughter which ensues, Lavinia, Tamora, Titus, and Saturninus all are slain. Lucius tells the people the true story of the persecutions of his father's house, and is proclaimed emperor. The Moor is condemned to a lingering death, half-buried in the sand.

NOTES

Titus Andronicus is one of the earlier works of Shakespeare, and by many is thought to be the earliest of all, dating back to 1589 or 1590. Langbaine, in his "English Dramatic Poets," mentions an edition of 1594; and Meres, in "Palladis Tamia," mentions it in 1598. Interval evidence is not reliable, as the play bears marks of more than one author. There is record, also, of possibly three plays being extant with the same name.

FIRST EDITIONS. The earliest Quarto now known is that of 1600. It does not bear Shakespeare's name, but states that it was acted, among others, by the "Lord Chamberlain's Servants" (Shakespeare's company). In 1611 another Quarto appeared using the same text, but still without stated authorship. The next edition now extant is that of the First Folio, of 1623, which first ascribes the play to Shakespeare. It also adds the second scene of Act III.

SOURCES. Although there were several early versions of *Titus Andronicus* by different hands, no common source for the play has as yet been found. It seems to have been popular as a story, and a stage version was known as early as 1584; but this is now lost. A ballad on the subject, published in Percy's "Reliques," in 1593, is now thought to have been condensed from the play.

ACTION. The stage action is limited to four days, with intervals. The historical period is indefinite, but belongs to the decline of the Roman Empire.

SELECTED CRITICISM. "This is the period of Shakespeare's tentative dramatic efforts. Among these, notwithstanding strong external evidence . . . it is difficult to admit *Titus Andronicus*. That tragedy belongs to the pre-Shakespearean school of bloody dramas. If any portion of it be from Shakespeare's hand, it has at least this interest —it shows that there was a period of Shakespeare's authorship when the Poet had not yet discovered himself, a period when he yielded to the popular influences of the day and hour; this much interest and no more."—DOWDEN.

ROMEO AND JULIET

Present play contains Prologue, 5 Acts, 24 Scenes, 2983 lines

CAST OF CHARACTERS

ESCALUS, *Prince of Verona*
PARIS, *a young nobleman, kinsman to the Prince*
MONTAGUE
CAPULET, } *heads of two houses at variance with each other*
An old man, cousin to Capulet
ROMEO, *son to Montague*
MERCUTIO, *kinsman to the Prince, and friend to Romeo*
BENVOLIO, *nephew to Montague, and friend to Romeo*
TYBALT, *nephew to Lady Capulet*
FRIAR LAURENCE,
FRIAR JOHN, } *Franciscans*
BALTHASAR, *servant to Romeo*
SAMPSON,
GREGORY, } *servants to Capulet*
PETER, *servant to Juliet's nurse*
ABRAHAM, *servant to Montague*
An Apothecary
Three Musicians
Page to Paris; another Page; an Officer
LADY MONTAGUE, *wife to Montague*
LADY CAPULET, *wife to Capulet*
JULIET, *daughter to Capulet*
Nurse to Juliet
*Citizens of Verona; Relations to both houses; Maskers, Guards,
    Watchmen, and Attendants*
Chorus

SCENE: *Verona; Mantua*

163

ACT I

The Veronese houses of Montague and Capulet have had a feud of long standing, which has brought about continued street brawls between retainers of the families, from the highest relatives to the lowest servants. The old Capulet gives a feast to which all his friends are bidden. Naturally the Montagues are not included in the list. But Romeo, the heir of the latter house, is persuaded to don a mask and present himself at the festivities, in order to catch a glimpse of Rosaline, a flame of his. Romeo, however, has scant eyes for Rosaline; he discovers another young girl whose beauty and grace set his heart beating as it never beat before. He inquires her name and is dismayed to learn that she is Juliet, the heiress of the Capulets. Meanwhile Tybalt, nephew to Lady Capulet, discovers the identity of Romeo, and is barely dissuaded by old Capulet—whose hospitality overrides his anger—from drawing upon the Montague.

ACT II

Juliet has likewise discovered the name of the handsome young stranger, who carried off her affections by storm at the banquet. Melancholy and lovelorn, she repairs to her balcony, and there confides to the moon and stars the secret of her heart. But it happens that Romeo is underneath the balcony and hears her confess her love for him. Overjoyed, he reveals his presence, and the maiden is constrained to make a further avowal. The lovers resolve on a speedy and secret marriage, which is brought to pass the very next day in the cell of Friar Laurence, a friend of Romeo's.

ACT III

On the day of the wedding two of Romeo's friends, Benvolio and Mercutio, while walking through the streets of Verona, are accosted by Tybalt, who is seeking an encounter with

Romeo because of the latter's presence at the Capulets' during the feast. A quarrel ensues, and at its height Romeo appears. Tybalt rails at him, but Romeo answers softly, for he is just returning from his wedding and the Capulets are no longer so hateful in his eyes. The others, however, cannot understand his weakness, and Mercutio, exasperated, fights Tybalt in his stead. Mercutio is slain. Romeo, in just vengeance, then turns upon and slays Tybalt. By a mandate of the Prince of Verona, Romeo is banished. He flees the land, leaving Juliet the weeping bride of one night.

Juliet's father, knowing nothing of her secret nuptials, is resolved to wed her to her kinsman, the young Paris.

ACT IV

In her despair Juliet consults the friendly Friar Laurence, who advises her to appear to consent to a marriage with Paris, but on her nuptial morn to drink a potion which the Friar prepares for her. This will give her, he says, the semblance of death; she will be laid away in the burial vault, and Romeo will be sent for to rescue her. She takes the drug as the Friar directs and her parents, heart-broken, believe her dead and consign her to the tomb.

ACT V

Bad news travels more swiftly than good. Before the Friar has had the opportunity to notify Romeo of the sham death, other messengers advise him that Juliet is really no more. Romeo, frantic with grief, procures a deadly poison and goes to Juliet's tomb to die beside his wife. At the door of the tomb he meets Paris, who forces him to fight. Paris is slain. Romeo enters the tomb, drinks the poison, and breathes his last. A few moments later Juliet awakes from her trance, sees her lover's dead body and learns the truth from Friar Laurence, who has but now arrived at the tomb. She seizes Romeo's dagger and kills herself. The double tragedy so affects the heads of the houses of

Capulet and Montague that they become reconciled as through a bloody sacrifice.

NOTES

Romeo and Juliet may be assigned to the earlier period of authorship between 1591 and 1596. It seems probable that the play was revised from an earlier or stage version about the latter date. This is clearly shown by textual evidence. As to external evidence, Weever in his "Epigrams," circa 1595, mentions Romeo as one of Shakespeare's popular characters and there are other local allusions linking it up with this period.

FIRST EDITIONS. The play first appeared incompletely in a Quarto, dated 1597, "as it hath been played by the Lord of Hunsdon's Servants." A second Quarto, in 1599, stated that it had been "publicly acted by the Lord Chamberlain's Servants." A third Quarto, 1609, bears the name of "W. Shakespeare," but not in all copies. This is the source of the First Folio version, of 1623.

SOURCES. The story of *Romeo and Juliet* occurs in varying form in Italian literature, both poetry and prose. It was popular with the troubadours. A version by Bandello, 1554, was translated into French by Boisteau, and thence into English by Arthur Brooke, in 1562. The Brooke poem seems to be the chief source of Shakespeare's play, although he probably was also familiar with a prose version of the story by Paynter, included in his "Palace of Pleasure" (1567).

ACTION. Shakespeare compressed a long-drawn-out story into four or five days, thus gaining much by the rapidity of tragic events. The historical period is indeterminate.

SELECTED CRITICISM. "Shakespeare did not intend to represent more than a fragment of human life in the tragedy. He did not aim at a criticism of the whole of human character; he cared to show us his hero and his heroine only as lovers, and as exemplary in the perfection of their love; faithful even unto death; choosing, with a final election of the heart, love at all costs. Here is no view of the whole of life; we are shown merely what befell a young pair of lovers during four days long ago in Verona."—DOWDEN.

TIMON OF ATHENS

⚜ ⚜ ⚜

Present play contains 5 Acts, 17 Scenes, 2335 lines

CAST OF CHARACTERS

TIMON, *a noble Athenian*

LUCIUS,
LUCULLUS, } *lords, hangers-on to Timon*
SEMPRONIUS,

VENTIDIUS, *one of Timon's false friends*

ALCIBIADES, *an Athenian captain*

APEMANTUS, *a churlish philosopher*

FLAVIUS, *steward to Timon*

FLAMINIUS,
LUCILIUS, } *servants to Timon*
SERVILIUS,

CAPHIS,
PHILOTUS,
TITUS, } *servants to Timon's creditors*
LUCIUS,
HORTENSIUS,

Poet
Painter
Jeweller
Merchant
An old Athenian
A Page
A Fool
Three Strangers

PHRYNIA,
TIMANDRA, } *mistresses to Alcibiades*

Cupid and Amazons in the mask

Other Lords, Senators, Officers, Soldiers, Banditti, and Attendants

SCENE: *Athens, and the neighbouring woods*

ACT I

The lavish generosity of Timon, a great lord of Athens, draws to him a throng of sycophants and hangers-on who profit by his careless extravagance. With his frank, cordial nature he does not suspect their true mission, but esteems them all his friends. They flatter him assiduously, and he showers gifts upon them or does them various good services. He gives a costly banquet at which the favours are precious stones. The reckless waste is a matter of much concern to his steward, who foresees speedy impoverishment.

ACT II

Presently Timon's creditors begin to suspect his true financial state and press him greatly with bills. The steward at last succeeds in acquainting his master with his bankrupt condition. Timon is thunderstruck, but consoles himself with the thought that he can draw upon all the men to whom he has been liberal in time past. He therefore despatches his servants to request from them loans.

ACT III

The false friends desert him in his hour of need; nor will they advance him money. Instead they make specious excuses and even go so far as to importune him in turn for certain sums. Timon's eyes are opened to their ingratitude and unworthiness. To express his contempt he gives a final feast, at which nothing is set forth but warm water. While uttering the bitterest reproaches he dashes the water in their faces, and ends by throwing the dishes at them and driving them out of the banqueting-room.

ACT IV

Timon now abjures the society of all mankind, and seeks refuge in a cave in the woods outside the city, where he subsists upon the roots of the earth. In digging them he discovers a hidden treasure of gold, but takes no pleasure in it, for it brings him only heavy recollections of his folly. He bestows a portion of the gold upon Alcibiades, a former friend of his who honestly desires to aid him, and who is now marching against Athens to humiliate that city for its unjust banishment of him. Though Timon wishes Alcibiades success, it is not because he is reconciled with him, but because he desires the punishment of Athens. The only man whom the misanthrope will acknowledge to be honest is his faithful steward, who seeks him out and remains true to him in adversity. Upon him Timon bestows a liberal gift of the treasure, enjoining him never to come within his sight again.

ACT V

The near approach of Alcibiades to Athens causes the senators to bethink themselves of the neglected Timon. They visit him in the forest to pray his aid, promising a restoration of fortune and honour. But Timon greets their advances with taunts and curses. They return bootless to the city, which they are shortly after forced to surrender to Alcibiades. While the conqueror is singling out his own and Timon's enemies for punishment, he receives word that Timon is dead within his forest cave.

NOTES

Timon of Athens has been assigned anywhere within the ten years following 1601. The difficulty as to date is occasioned by the facts that there were no early editions of the play; no contemporary mentions of it; and the play is now thought to be only partly by Shakespeare.

FIRST EDITION.   The First Folio, of 1623, included the play for the first time in printed form. The text is full of errors and obscurities, and since there is no other version, editors have experienced considerable difficulty with it.

SOURCES.   Plutarch's "Lives" contains in the Life of Antonius a short account of Timon. Another account was given by Paynter in his "Palace of Pleasure." Other allusions have been found in literature, but the above two are the most nearly related to the Shakespearean version.

ACTION.   The stage time of the play is six days, with one long interval occurring in Act IV. The historical period is indefinite.

SELECTED CRITICISM.   "The play of *Timon* is a domestic tragedy, and therefore strongly fastens on the attention of the reader. In the plan there is not much art, but the incidents are natural, and the characters various and exact. The catastrophe affords a very powerful warning against that ostentatious liberality, which scatters bounty, but confers no benefits, and brings flattery but not friendship. In this tragedy are many passages perplexed, obscure, and probably corrupt, which I have endeavored to rectify, or explain, with due diligence; but having only one copy, cannot promise myself that my endeavors shall be much applauded."—SAMUEL JOHNSON.

JULIUS CÆSAR

❧ ❧ ❧

Present play contains 5 Acts, 18 Scenes, 2422 lines

CAST OF CHARACTERS

JULIUS CÆSAR, *a Roman general*

OCTAVIUS CÆSAR, MARK ANTONY, M. ÆMILIUS LEPIDUS, *triumvirs after death of Julius Cæsar*

CICERO, PUBLIUS, POPILIUS LENA, *senators*

MARCUS BRUTUS, CASSIUS, CASCA, TREBONIUS, LIGARIUS, DECIUS BRUTUS, METELLUS CIMBER, CINNA, *conspirators against Julius Cæsar*

FLAVIUS, MARULLUS, *tribunes*

ARTEMIDORUS, *of Cnidos, a teacher of rhetoric*

A Soothsayer

CINNA, *a poet*

Another poet

LUCILIUS, TITINIUS, MESSALA, *Young* CATO VOLUMNIUS, *friends to Brutus and Cassius*

VARRO, CLITUS, CLAUDIUS, STRATO, LUCIUS, DARDANIUS, *servants to Brutus*

PINDARUS, *servant to Cassius*

CALPURNIA, *wife to Cæsar*

PORTIA, *wife to Brutus*

Senators, Citizens, Guards, Attendants, and others

SCENE: *Rome; near Sardis; near Philippi*

ACT I

Julius Cæsar returns victorious from foreign wars and, according to custom, the citizens of Rome escort him in triumph to the Capitol. So overjoyed are they that Mark Antony deems the day propitious to offer him a kingly crown. This is thrice offered and thrice refused. But even in the hour of Cæsar's greatest triumph forces are at work against him. Cassius has gathered together a band of conspirators, who finally persuade Brutus, a high-minded Roman, to join them, under the belief that the death of Cæsar will be for the country's good.

ACT II

Upon his entry into Rome, Cæsar had been warned by a sooth-sayer to "beware the ides of March." So on the dawn of this portentous day, he is minded to remain at home, especially since his wife has been the victim of ominous dreams. But the con-spirators have foreseen his hesitancy and therefore come in a body to urge his attendance at the senate-house. Ashamed of his fears, he yields and goes with them.

ACT III

Once in the senate-house, the conspirators, under guise of pre-senting a petition, press about Cæsar; and presently each one stabs him, Brutus thrusting last of all. Cæsar murmurs, *"Et tu, Brute?"* and expires.

Mark Antony, Cæsar's steadfast friend, flies at the first scent of danger, but returns to dissemble with the slayers of Cæsar. He pleads friendliness for their cause, but begs permission to speak at the burial of the slain leader. Brutus generously con-sents to this, despite his friends' disapproval, stipulating only that he himself speak first, and that Antony in his oration make no charges. Antony declares himself satisfied. Brutus accord-ingly makes a short speech to the citizens, in which he pleads the general welfare as sufficient cause and excuse for the slay-ing of Cæsar. Antony follows him in a skilful harangue, full of praise for Cæsar; and though referring to Brutus and his party as "honourable men," he turns the term into a reproach and byword. The populace, which but a moment before was ap-plauding Brutus to the echo, now turns in fury against him. The conspirators are forced to flee the city.

ACT IV

Upon the death of Cæsar two factions arise and take the field against each other. The first is the army of Brutus and Cassius. The second comprises the forces of a newly formed triumvirate, consisting of Mark Antony, Octavius Cæsar, and Lepidus. Both armies converge towards the Plains of Philippi. One night while Brutus is lying awake and restless in his tent the ghost of Cæsar appears and tells him, "Thou shalt see me at Philippi."

ACT V

The forces meet at Philippi and engage in battle. But from the first the troops of Brutus and Cassius are dispirited—unconsciously influenced by the forebodings that have come to both their leaders. With his own "good sword, that ran through Cæsar's bowels," Cassius causes himself to be killed by his servant Pindarus. Later in the day Brutus runs on his sword and dies. The triumvirate are victorious, and Cæsar may "now be still."

NOTES

Several early commentators place *Julius Cæsar* in the year 1607, but more recent critics are inclined to an earlier time coincident with *Hamlet,* or about 1601. Weever's "Mirror of Martyrs" contains a reference to Brutus' speech (1601) "that Cæsar was ambitious," which would seem to indicate the present play. Drayton's "The Barrons War," revised in 1603, contains a suggestion of Antony's closing speech.

FIRST EDITION. The earliest printed version that has come down to us is that of the First Folio, of 1623. The text is printed with great care, and may have come directly from the author's revised manuscript. The play is listed in the "Stationers' Register," for that year, as not having previously been entered to other men.

SOURCES.   Plutarch's "Lives," as translated by Sir Thomas North, was the chief source of historical material—particularly the lives of Cæsar, Brutus, and Antony. The dramatist not only obtained here the facts as to their lives but also many of the speeches themselves, which he paraphrased in poetic form. Shakespeare, however, adds the orations of Brutus and Antony and compresses the action into more dramatic form.

ACTION.   Six days are depicted on the stage, with suggested intervals between scenes. The historical period extends from Cæsar's entry into Rome, 45 B. C., to the Battle of Philippi, three years later.

SELECTED CRITICISM.   "The style of *Julius Cæsar* is characterized by simplicity and breadth of touch; and each sentence is clear, easy and flowing, with the thought clothed in perfect and adequate expression. The lives are as limpid as those of *Romeo and Juliet,* but without their remains of rhyme and Italian conceits. Of all Shakespeare's works, none has greater purity of verse or transparent fluency. . . . Nothing perhaps in the whole roll of dramatic poetry equals the tenderness given by Shakespeare to Brutus, that tenderness of a strong nature which the force of contrast renders so touching and so beautiful."—STAPFER.

MACBETH

❧ ❧ ❧

Present play contains 5 Acts, 27 Scenes, 2085 lines

CAST OF CHARACTERS

DUNCAN, *King of Scotland*

MALCOLM,
DONALBAIN, } *sons to Duncan*

MACBETH,
BANQUO, } *generals of the King's army*

MADCUFF,
LENNOX,
ROSS,
MENTEITH, } *noblemen of Scotland*
ANGUS,
CAITHNESS,

FLEANCE, *son to Banquo*

SIWARD, *Earl of Northumberland, general of the English forces*

YOUNG SIWARD, *son to Siward*

SEYTON, *an officer attending on Macbeth*

BOY, *son to Macduff*

A Scotch Doctor　　　　　　*An English Doctor*

A Porter　　　　　　　　　*A Soldier*

An Old Man

LADY MACBETH, *wife to Macbeth*

LADY MACDUFF, *wife to Macduff*

Gentlewoman attending on Lady Macbeth

HECATE

Three Witches

Apparitions

*Lords, Gentlemen, Officers, Soldiers, Murderers, Attendants
and Messengers*

SCENE: *Scotland; England*

175

ACT I

Macbeth and Banquo, two commanding generals under King Duncan of Scotland, achieve a signal victory over a rebel army, although the latter is supported by Norwegian troops. On their return from battle the two Scottish generals are accosted by three witches, who hail Macbeth as Thane of Glamis, Thane of Cawdor, and future King of Scotland. Afterwards they promise Banquo that his sons shall sit upon the throne. Macbeth is already Thane of Glamis, but nothing more. While the witches' announcement is yet sounding in his ears, messengers from the King arrive and confer upon him, in Duncan's name, and because of his victory, the title of Thane of Cawdor. This verification of two terms of the witches' greeting leads Macbeth secretly to hope for the third—the throne itself. He communicates this wish to his wife, a cruel, unscrupulous woman, and their joint desire develops into a plot against the King. The monarch, suspecting nothing, seeks to do Macbeth still further honour by visiting him.

ACT II

During the visit the King is murdered by Macbeth, aided by his wife. Malcolm and Donalbain, the King's sons, flee the country in terror; and Macbeth seeks to divert suspicion concerning the deed from himself to them. Since the sons have fled, Macbeth, as next heir, is crowned King of Scotland. The third prediction of the witches is accomplished, though at a price of blood.

ACT III

Macbeth, however, is unsatisfied. He bethinks himself that Banquo also was promised something by the Weird Sisters—namely, that his children shall one day mount the throne. The thought is galling to Macbeth, who wishes to make the crown secure for his own posterity. He plots to kill Banquo and his only son, Fleance. To further the plot he makes a great feast and invites Banquo and Fleance particularly. On their way thither they are way-laid and Banquo is slain by murderers in Macbeth's employ, but Fleance escapes.

While the slain Banquo's blood is yet warm and flowing, Macbeth's feast is spread. It is indeed a regal repast, and King Macbeth himself says that but one feature is lacking—the presence of his chief guest, Banquo. This he says to divert suspicion, for he has already received news of Banquo's violent end. But scarcely has he uttered the words when the ghost of Banquo appears at Macbeth's seat. No one sees him save Macbeth, but his alarm causes the banquet to break up in confusion.

ACT IV

Macbeth, harried by doubts and fears, resolves upon and obtains another interview with the witches. He is warned to beware of Macduff; he is promised that "none of woman born shall harm Macbeth"; he is advised to fear naught till Birnam wood shall come against him. Still unsatisfied, he demands again to know if Banquo's issue shall reign in the kingdom, and from what the witches show he becomes convinced that the crown is assigned to them. The first news that greets him upon leaving the witches is that Macduff has escaped to England to join forces with Malcolm, the late king's eldest son. Enraged, Macbeth storms Macduff's castle and puts Lady Macduff and her children to the sword.

ACT V

The Queen meanwhile is almost insane over the thought of her own share in Macbeth's crimes. She walks in her sleep and endeavours to wash imaginary blood-stains from her hands. Finally she expires, "as 'tis thought, by self and violent hands."

Macbeth also is growing tired of life, but the hag's last prophecies spur him to renewed effort. He is almost unmanned, therefore, when word is brought that Birnam wood is moving against him; for this was one of the apparently impossible threats of the witches. The moving woods are really branches of the trees of Birnam lopped off and carried by the invading troops of Malcolm and Macduff to protect their advance against him. Still Macbeth believes himself invulnerable, and fearing none save one "that was not born of woman," he rushes forth to battle. He fights with almost superhuman strength and valour till he meets Macduff, against whom he remembers that he has been warned by the witches. At first he shrinks from fighting Macduff, but when brought to bay, exclaims: "I bear a charmed life, which must not yield to one of woman born." "Despair thy charm," retorts his foe, "Macduff was from his mother's womb untimely ripp'd." And in the ensuing duel Macbeth is slain. Malcolm is hailed King of Scotland.

NOTES

The year 1606 is a probable date for *Macbeth*. We know that it was written after 1603, through an allusion to the union of England and Scotland; and before 1610, as Dr. Simon Forman mentions it that year in his Diary. In 1607, "The Puritan" appeared with a probable reference to Banquo's ghost. Internal evidence supports this date of 1606.

FIRST EDITION. The play was first published in the First Folio, of 1623. The text is more than usually faulty, and as there are no parallel Quartos, succeeding editors have had great difficulty in untangling doubtful passages.

SOURCES. The historical background for *Macbeth* is found in two stories from Holinshed's "Chronicles." Shakespeare may also have been aided either directly or indirectly by Thomas Middleton, whose play "The Witch" contains scenes and passages similar to the witch portion of *Macbeth*.

ACTION. The historical period extends about twenty years. Duncan was slain about 1040, and Macbeth about 1060. The stage time is nine days, with various intervals suggested between scenes.

SELECTED CRITICISM. "This drama shows us the gathering, the discharge, and the dispelling of a domestic and political storm, which takes its peculiar view from the individual character of the hero. It is not in the spirit of mischief that animates the 'weird sisters,' nor in the passionate and strong-willed ambition of Lady Macbeth, that we find the mainspring of this tragedy, but in the disproportioned though poetically tempered soul of Macbeth himself."
—FLETCHER.

HAMLET, PRINCE OF DENMARK

❧ ❧ ❧

Present play contains 5 Acts, 20 Scenes, 3777 lines

CAST OF CHARACTERS

CLAUDIUS, *King of Denmark*
HAMLET, *son to the late, and nephew to the present King*
HORATIO, *friend to Hamlet*   POLONIUS, *Lord Chamberlain*
LAERTES, *son to Polonius*

VOLTIMAND,
CORNELIUS,
ROSENCRANTZ, ⎫ *courtiers*
GUILDENSTERN,
OSRIC,

A Gentleman
A Priest

MARCELLUS, ⎫ *officers*
BERNARDO, ⎭

FRANCISCO, *a soldier*   REYNALDO, *servant to Polonius*
Players   *A Captain*
Ambassadors   FORTINBRAS, *Prince of Norway*
Two Clowns, grave-diggers
GERTRUDE, *Queen of Denmark, and mother to Hamlet*
OPHELIA, *daughter to Polonius*
Ghost of Hamlet's father
Lords, Ladies, Officers, Soldiers, Sailors, Messengers, and At-
    tendants

SCENE: *Elsinore, Denmark*

ACT I

Hamlet, Prince of Denmark, is advised by the sentinels of the
royal castle of Kronborg, at Elsinore, that an apparition strongly

resembling his dead father had appeared on the battlements. Hamlet therefore resolves to encounter the spirit and learn from it, if possible, the true cause of his father's taking-off, about which the Prince has had many suspicions. He meets the Ghost at its next nightly visitation, and in an interview with it his worst fears are confirmed. The late King's brother Claudius, who has ascended the throne and wedded the widowed Queen, had poisoned the King while he slept. Hamlet is enjoined to secrecy and revenge, and the Ghost vanishes. Hamlet's followers are sworn to say nothing of the occurrence.

ACT II

Because of the news and of the dread task to which he is commissioned, Hamlet is seized with a species of madness, perhaps largely feigned, whereby he may cloak his designs. He writes incoherent and passionate letters to his lady-love, Ophelia, daughter of Polonius, a court dignitary. At this juncture a company of strolling players arrives at the castle and at Hamlet's suggestion a certain play is given before the King and Queen and members of the court.

ACT III

The play deals with the murder of a Venetian duke, whose wife afterwards weds the murderer. The story closely resembles the circumstances of the King of Denmark's demise. During the play Hamlet is intent not upon the players but upon the countenance and actions of his uncle. The latter, as if struck with a realising sense of his own crime, as Hamlet suspected, hurriedly leaves. Hamlet no longer doubts the truth of the Ghost's communications, and turns with energy to seek the vengeance which he has sworn to execute.

The queen mother is also much disturbed by the purport of the play, and sends for Hamlet in order to upbraid him. Hamlet answers reproach with reproach, and leaves his mother overwhelmed with shame and self-convicted. But for the opportune arrival of the dead King's spirit, Hamlet might have adopted even more violent measures. Ophelia's father, Polonius, who is spying upon this interview, is slain by Hamlet, who mistakes him for the King.

ACT IV

Hamlet's banishment is decided upon. Two former school comrades of his are entrusted with a commission to leave him in England, where sealed orders are to bring about the Prince's death. But by a combination of plot and accident the execution is visited instead upon the heads of the two accomplices. Hamlet returns to Denmark. There he is greeted by a strange spectacle—the funeral of a young girl, honoured by the presence of the King, Queen, and persons of the court. Hamlet has in fact arrived home just at the time of Ophelia's interment. That unfortunate maiden, through incessant brooding over the madness of her lover, the untimely end of her father, and the continued absence of her brother, Laertes, had become insane. For some days she had wandered about the court singing and strewing flowers, then had strayed to the banks of a stream and been drowned.

ACT V

When Hamlet discovers that it is Ophelia's funeral, he is beside himself with grief. He leaps into the grave and angrily contests with Laertes, who also has just returned, the place of chief mourner. Laertes in turn desires to kill Hamlet, for he regards the Prince as the cause of all the woes that have fallen upon his house.

Seeing the animosity of Laertes, King Claudius thinks he may make use of it to work Hamlet's undoing. He secretly advises Laertes to engage Hamlet in a fencing-match—supposedly friendly. Laertes' foil, however, is to be naked and envenomed. Hamlet, unsuspecting, consents to a trial of skill before the court. The King prepares a poisoned drink for Hamlet, if perchance he shall escape the tipped foil. Laertes and Hamlet fence. After a touch or two for Hamlet, the Queen, to do him honour, toasts him—unwittingly—with the poisoned cup. Laertes wounds Hamlet. In the scuffle they change rapiers, and Hamlet in turn wounds Laertes with the latter's treacherous blade. The Queen dies from the drugged wine. Lærtes falls, but before he dies he confesses his guilty design and craves pardon of the Prince. Hamlet turns upon the King with his own dying strength and stabs the usurping monarch to the heart.

NOTES

Hamlet was probably written between the years 1598 and 1602. It is not mentioned by Meres in his "Palladis Tamia" of the earlier year; and in the latter year it was entered in the "Stationers' Register." Internal evidence places it about the year 1600.

FIRST EDITIONS. In 1603 an imperfect text of *Hamlet,* evidently a pirated version, was published. The next year a clearer, and doubtless official, text was printed, now called the Second Quarto. Both had Shakespeare's name on the title page. The Third Quarto appeared in 1605, and the Fourth in 1611. The First Folio, of 1623, supplies some additional readings not found in any Quarto.

SOURCES. In the twelfth century, the "Historia Danica" by Saxo Grammaticus, a Danish writer of importance, contained the story of Hamlet. The story went the rounds of the minstrels and story-tellers, and was first printed in 1514. Belleforest translated it into French in his "Histoires Tragiques," of 1571. Shakespeare may have been familiar with the story aside from either printed form. An earlier play of "Hamlet," now lost, was known to his company of players, about 1590.

ACTION. The historical period is indeterminate, but dates back to the eighth or tenth century. The time depicted on the stage is seven days, with intervals considerably lengthening this time.

SELECTED CRITICISM. *"Hamlet* is a name; his speeches and sayings but the idle coinage of the poet's brain. What then, are they not real? They are as real as our own thoughts. Their reality is in the reader's mind. It is we who are Hamlet. This play has a prophetic truth, which is above that of history. Whoever has become thoughtful and melancholy through his own mishaps or those of others; whoever has borne about with him the clouded brow of reflection and thought himself 'too much i' th' sun' . . . this is the true Hamlet." —HAZLITT.

KING LEAR

⚜ ⚜ ⚜

Present play contains 5 Acts, 25 Scenes, 3102 lines

CAST OF CHARACTERS

LEAR, *King of Britain*
KING OF FRANCE
DUKE OF BURGUNDY
DUKE OF CORNWALL
DUKE OF ALBANY
EARL OF KENT
EARL OF GLOUCESTER
EDGAR, *son to Gloucester*
EDMUND, *natural son to Gloucester*
CURAN, *a courtier*
Old Man, tenant to Gloucester
Doctor
Fool
OSWALD, *steward to Goneril*
A Captain employed by Edmund
Gentlemen attendant on Cordelia
A Herald
Servants to Cornwall
GONERIL, ⎫
REGAN, ⎬ *daughters to Lear*
CORDELIA, ⎭
Knights of Lear's train, Captains, Messengers, Soldiers, and
  Attendants

SCENE: *Britain*

ACT I

Lear, King of Britain, being desirous of escaping the cares of
state on account of advancing years, determines to portion out

183

his kingdom among his three daughters, Goneril, Regan, and Cordelia. In his old age he craves expressions of his daughters' affection. Both Goneril and Regan make most eloquent protestations of their love; and the delighted monarch forthwith bestows on each a third of his kingdom. But Cordelia, disgusted with such lip service, will not please her father by like avowals, but promises only to love him according to her duty. Lear, enraged, takes away her moiety of the realm and divides it between Goneril and Regan. The Earl of Kent interposes on behalf of Cordelia, and is himself banished. Though dowerless, Cordelia's hand is sought and obtained by the King of France.

It is not long before Lear discovers that he has been disappointed in his estimate of the two elder daughters. By agreement, he had reserved nothing more than the title of king, and a retinue of one hundred knights. He was to spend alternately a month at the courts of Goneril and Regan.

ACT II

These undutiful daughters, however, reduce the size of his train, cavil at the moderate demands made upon them, give him grudging maintenance, and conspire to drive him into open rupture with them.

ACT III

Finally, after a passionate scene, the old King betakes himself to the desolate heath on a stormy night, where he braves the fury of the elements. He is accompanied by the two remaining retainers of his court—his jester and the Earl of Kent, who has returned from banishment to serve him in disguise. The three take refuge in a hovel, where they encounter a supposed madman—Edgar, the disguised son of the Earl of Gloucester, who had been supplanted in his father's affections by his natural half-brother, Edmund. Lear's mind becomes unbalanced. In his extremity the Earl of Gloucester ministers to him. The treacherous Edmund informs Regan and Goneril of the kindness, and Cornwall, Regan's husband, tears out Gloucester's eyes.

ACT IV

Shortly after, while being led in his blindness on the heath, Gloucester is met and recognised by his disowned son Edgar, who, unknown to his father, takes him under his protection and cures Gloucester of his suicidal mania.

Meanwhile, Cordelia, learning through Kent of her sisters' treachery and the ensuing plight of her father, comes to his relief with a French army. She nurses him, and endeavours to restore him to sanity.

ACT V

A battle is fought between Cordelia's French troops, and the English forces under the command of Edmund, who holds equivocal relations towards both Goneril and Regan. Cordelia's army is defeated and herself and Lear taken prisoners. Goneril —for Edmund's sake—poisons her sister Regan; and afterwards when her husband discovers her perfidy, stabs herself. Edmund is killed in a combat with his wronged brother, Edgar. By an order of Edmund, too late countermanded, Cordelia is hanged in prison, and Lear dies broken-hearted at this last calamity.

NOTES

King Lear can be assigned very closely to the year 1605. It was entered in the "Stationers' Register" in 1607, and mentioned as having been performed the preceding Christmas. A reference in the text to the "late eclipses" is believed to refer to an eclipse of the sun in 1605.

FIRST EDITIONS. Two Quarto editions appeared in 1608, both bearing Shakespeare's name on the title page, and with lengthy inscriptions about the play and its players. The First Folio, of 1623, gives a different text in many respects from the Quartos. It is also freer from printer's errors.

SOURCES. The story of "Leir, the son of Balderd" is one of the earliest and best known of British history. Its first printed form was in the "Historia Britonum," a Latin work of the twelfth century. Several other versions of the tale followed up to Shakespeare's day, the one just preceding his own work being a drama acted in 1594, entitled, "The True Chronicle History of King Leir and his three daughters, Gonorill, Ragan, and Cordella." The author's name was not given. This play bears little resemblance to Shakespeare's, however.

ACTION. The stage representation is about ten days, with intervals suggesting a month's total time. It is impossible to give any historical period for the play, as the setting is legendary.

SELECTED CRITICISM. "The Lear of Shakespeare cannot be acted. The contemptible machinery by which they mimic the storm which he goes out in, is not more inadequate to represent the horrors of the real elements, than any actor can be to represent Lear; they might more easily propose to personate the Satan of Milton upon a stage, or one of Michael Angelo's terrible figures. The greatness of Lear is not in corporal dimension, but in intellectual; the explosions of his passion are terrible as a volcano; they are storms turning up and disclosing to the bottom that sea his mind, with all its vast riches. It is his mind which is laid bare."—CHARLES LAMB.

OTHELLO

THE MOOR OF VENICE

Present play contains 5 Acts, 15 Scenes, 3202 lines

CAST OF CHARACTERS

DUKE OF VENICE
BRABANTIO, *a senator*
Other Senators
GRATIANO, *brother to Brabantio*
LODOVICO, *kinsman to Brabantio*
OTHELLO, *a noble Moor, in the service of the Venetian state*
CASSIO, *lieutenant to Othello*
IAGO, *ancient to Othello*
Clown, servant to Othello
RODERIGO, *a Venetian gentleman*
MONTANO, *Othello's predecessor in the government of Cyprus*
DESDEMONA, *daughter to Brabantio, and wife to Othello*
EMILIA, *wife to Iago*
BIANCA, *mistress to Cassio*
*Sailor, Messenger, Herald, Officers, Gentlemen, Musicians, and
    Attendants*
SCENE: *Venice; a Seaport in Cyprus*

ACT I

Desdemona, a beautiful and high-born Venetian maiden, is
wooed and won by Othello, a Moorish general, whose dusky
skin cannot conceal a chivalrous and adventurous spirit such as
women love. Desdemona's father, Brabantio, learning of their
secret marriage, is much incensed and goes before the Duke of
Venice and complains that his daughter has been stolen from

him. But it so happens that Othello's warlike qualities are in
demand upon the very night in which these affairs culminate.
He has been in the service of the Venetian government, and the
state now requires his presence in Cyprus to oppose a Turkish
fleet. He is therefore suffered to depart in peace with his wife
Desdemona, especially since she, in the council chamber, declares
her love and confidence in him.

ACT II

Iago, Othello's ancient or ensign, has sworn secret enmity against
his master because the Moor raised Cassio instead of himself to the chief lieutenancy. The enmity has taken the form of
carefully laid plots, which began with the very nuptial night
of Othello. In Cyprus, whither Othello and his train repair,
the plots have abundant time for ripening. A storm has wrecked
the Turkish fleet, and Othello remains in command on land
amid a general revelry, authorised by him, to celebrate the
dispersion of the enemy and in honour of his own nuptials.
During the feasting Iago makes Cassio drunk and involves him
in a street brawl. Othello arrives on the scene and deprives the
officer of his lieutenancy.

ACT III

Iago advises Cassio to sue for favour and restoration of rank
through Desdemona, since Othello will deny her nothing. Cassio,
unsuspicious of treachery, obtains an interview with her, and
Iago lures Othello to the scene—innocent enough, but greeted
by Iago with an ominous shake of the head. Othello, seeing
the gesture, questions his ensign, whereupon the latter instils
the poison of jealousy into his master's ears, making him to
doubt Desdemona's relations with Cassio. The doubt is in-
tensified when that lady, in the kindness of her heart, intercedes
for Cassio. Henceforward Iago loses no opportunity to add to
his master's jealousy. He procures by stealth a handkerchief
given by Othello to Desdemona, and causes it to be found in
Cassio's possession.

ACT IV

Othello becomes convinced that his wife has been untrue to him. He determines upon her death, and charges his supposed friend Iago with the task of despatching Cassio. Nothing loth, Iago embroils Cassio in a night combat with Roderigo, a former suitor of Desdemona's, entangled in the meshes of Iago.

ACT V

Cassio wounds Roderigo. Iago desires the death of both, and so unseen, stabs Cassio. Meanwhile Othello goes to Desdemona's bedchamber and smothers her to death. Emilia, the wife of Iago and devoted servant of Desdemona, proves to Othello that the wife he has just murdered is innocent. Iago kills Emilia. Othello wounds Iago, then kills himself. Cassio, who still lives, is advanced to the government of Cyprus. Iago is reserved for lingering torture.

NOTES

Othello is rather definitely assigned to the year 1604. An account in the "Court Revels" states that it was acted in that year. The first acting version as printed in the Quarto contained many oaths which the First Folio omitted. An Act of Parliament against profanity in plays took effect in 1606.

FIRST EDITIONS. A Quarto was published in 1622, or only one year prior to the First Folio. Both ascribed the play to Shakespeare, but the Folio version is longer and clearer in its readings than the other, so must have been derived from another source.

SOURCES. The story of "The Moor of Venice" is found in an Italian group by Giraldi Cinthio, the "Heccatommithi." A French version of this book came out in 1584. The chief facts as to the four or five leading characters of Shakespeare's play are found in Cinthio's tale, but only in outline. The thought and dramatic interplay of *Othello* are the dramatist's own.

ACTION.   The stage time represented is three or four days, with intervals suggested to allow for the more gradual unfolding of the plot. The historical period may be assigned to the year 1570, when the Turks attacked Cyprus.

SELECTED CRITICISM.   "Were *Othello* but the spirited portrait of a half-tamed barbarian, we should view him as a bold and happy poetical conception. . . . But it is because it depicts a noble mind, wrought by deep passion and dark devices to agonies such as every one might feel, that it awakens our strongest sympathies. We see in this drama a grand and true moral picture; we read in it a profound ethical lesson; for while the matchless work is built up to the noblest height of poetry, it rests upon the deepest foundations of true philosophy."—VERPLANCK.

ANTONY AND CLEOPATRA

❦ ❦ ❦

Present play contains 5 Acts, 41 Scenes, 3024 lines

CAST OF CHARACTERS

MARK ANTONY, OCTAVIUS CÆSAR, M. ÆMILIUS LEPIDUS, *triumvirs*

SEXTUS POMPEIUS

DOMITIUS ENOBARBUS, VENTIDIUS, EROS, SCARUS, DERCETAS, DEMETRIUS, PHILO, *friends to Antony*

MECÆNAS, AGRIPPA, DOLABELLA, PROCULEIUS, THYREUS, GALLUS, *friends to Cæsar*

MENAS, MENECRATES, VARRIUS, *friends to Pompey*

TAURUS, *lieutenant-general to Cæsar*

CANIDIUS, *lieutenant-general to Antony*

SILIUS, *an officer in Ventidius's army*

EUPHRONIUS, *an ambassador from Antony to Cæsar*

ALEXAS; MARDIAN, *a eunuch;* SELEUCUS; DIOMEDES, *attendants on Cleopatra*

A Soothsayer

A Clown

CLEOPATRA, *Queen of Egypt*

OCTAVIA, *sister to Cæsar, and wife to Antony*

CHARMIAN, IRAS, *attendants on Cleopatra*

Officers, Soldiers, Messengers, and other Attendants

  SCENE: *In various parts of the Roman Empire*

ACT I

After the defeat of Brutus and Cassius at Philippi, the Roman Empire had been divided among the triumvirs, Antony, Octavius, and Lepidus. Antony having summoned a vassal of his Eastern dominions—Cleopatra, Queen of Egypt—to answer for her conduct in aiding Brutus and Cassius, is himself taken

191

captive by her charms. He goes with her to Alexandria, where they give themselves over to the voluptuous life of her court. A messenger arrives to inform Antony of the death of his deserted wife Fulvia. Another messenger brings him word of an attack upon Italy by the maritime forces of Sextus Pompeius. Antony shakes off his amorous chains despite Cleopatra's passion, and hastens back to the seat of empire.

ACT II

Antony reaches Rome just in time to patch up serious differences with the other two triumvirs, to whom he explains the attack upon Italy as merely a feint on the part of his late wife Fulvia to recall him from Egypt. He renews alliance with the other triumvirs by marrying Octavia, the sister of Octavius. A treaty of peace is made between the triumvirate and Pompey.

ACT III

Octavia, instead of serving as a bond to the friendship of Octavius and Antony, becomes a knot to strangle it; for Octavius soon breaks his peace with Pompey, defeats him in battle, and presently seizes Lepidus, whom he holds in prison. None now remains between Octavius and absolute dominion save Antony, who might have proved a strong rival had not the enticements of Cleopatra lured him once more over sea, while his wife is on a mission of peace to Octavius, who, no doubt, is incensed because of the treatment his sister has received, but is also glad to have this pretext for attacking Antony. The hostile fleets engage near Actium, where the defection of Cleopatra's admiral gives the victory to Octavius. Antony seeks to make terms with the victor, but being unsuccessful, hurls defiance at him.

ACT IV

The forces now encounter upon land, and Antony wins the first day's fight. But on the second day the Egyptian admiral yields

Antony's fleet to the foe, and the desertion of other of Antony's forces leaves him defeated, disheartened, and dishonoured. In a stormy scene he upbraids Cleopatra with treachery, and soon after falls upon his sword. He dies in her presence, begging to lay his last kiss upon her lips.

ACT V

Cleopatra, who, despite her duplicity, has been passionately engrossed with Antony and his fortunes, determines to follow him to speedy death. Her purpose is strengthened by the fact that Octavius makes her a hostage of war, and reserves her to grace his triumph. She flees to a monument, and there perishes by the bite of an asp secretly brought to her in a basket of figs.

NOTES

Antony and Cleopatra was entered for publication in 1608, although not actually brought out then. Internal evidence based on line endings and metre show it to belong to the same group with *Cymbeline* and *The Tempest,* or about 1607–1608.

FIRST EDITION.   There is no record of the play's performance and no printed version prior to the First Folio, of 1623. As mentioned above, an entry of the play was made in 1608, but no Quarto was issued. The Folio text, however, seems to have followed a carefully edited version and is on the whole satisfactory.

SOURCES.   Plutarch's "Lives," the North version, gave the dramatist, in the "Life of Marcus Antonius," a rich vein of material. Not only were historical facts used, but also many passages and speeches. Shakespeare, however, wove the material into poetic and dramatic beauty. The subject of Cleopatra was a favorite one in many lands, and at least two English plays antedated Shakespeare with this heroine; but they are dissimilar to his work.

ACTION.   The historical period extends from the Battle of Philippi (following *Julius Cæsar chronologically*) 42 B. C., to the deaths of

Antony and the Egyptian Queen, 30 B. C. The stage time is twelve days, with frequent intervals indicated.

SELECTED CRITICISM. "On *Antony and Cleopatra* Shakespeare has poured out the glory of his genius in profusion, and makes us stand by, saddened and distressed, as the noble Antony sinks to his ruin, under the gorgeous coloring of the Eastern sky, the vicious splendor of the Egyptian Queen; makes us look with admiring hate on the wonderful picture he has drawn, certainly far the most wonderful study of woman he has left us. . . . How admirably transferred from Plutarch's prose! And how that fatal inability to say 'No' to woman shows us Antony's weakness and the cause of his final fall."
—FURNIVALL.

PERICLES

PRINCE OF TYRE

Present play contains 5 Prologues, 1 Epilogue, 5 Acts, 22 Scenes, 2357 lines

CAST OF CHARACTERS

ANTIOCHUS, *King of Antioch*
PERICLES, *Prince of Tyre*
HELICANUS, ⎱ *two lords of Tyre*
ESCANES, ⎰
SIMONIDES, *King of Pentapolis*
CLEON, *Governor of Tarsus*
LYSIMACHUS, *Governor of Mytilene*
CERIMON, *a lord of Ephesus*
THALIARD, *a lord of Antioch*
PHILEMON, *servant to Cerimon*
LEONINE, *servant to Dionyza*
Marshal
A Pander
BOULT, *servant to Pander*
The Daughter of Antiochus
DIONYZA, *wife to Cleon*
THAISA, *daughter to Simonides*
MARINA, *daughter to Pericles and Thaisa*
LYCHORIDA, *nurse to Mariana*
A Courtesan
Lords, Knights, Gentlemen, Sailors, Pirates, Fishermen, and Messengers
DIANA
GOWER, *as Chorus*

SCENE: *In various countries*

ACT I

Antiochus, King of Antioch, in order to keep his daughter un-
married, for a shameful purpose, subjects to the penalty of
death all her suitors who do not succeed in solving a certain
riddle. After many have perished in the endeavour to win the
beautiful but wicked princess, Pericles, Prince of Tyre, ex-
pounds the riddle, which carries with it the story of Antiochus's
sin. To prevent the divulging of the secret, the monarch seeks
to have Pericles put to death. The latter flees to his own kingdom, whither Antiochus's wrath pursues him in the shape of
a plot to poison him. But Pericles anticipates this by continuing
his flight into other lands. He touches at Tarsus, where his
provisioned ships bring relief to that famine-stricken city.

ACT II

Pericles is afterwards driven by a storm on the shore of Pentapolis, and suffers a shipwreck, which he alone survives. Hearing that Simonides, the King of the country, is giving a tourna-
ment in honour of his daughter Thaisa, he goes to the court,
engages in the exercises, and creates so favourable an impression that, though he is poor and unknown, the princess chooses
him for her husband, and the King ratifies the nuptials.

ACT III

Several months later, word reaches Pericles that his ancient
enemy, Antiochus, is dead; also that his presence is needed to
maintain his crown at Tyre. He reveals his identity to his wife
and royal father-in-law, and embarks with Thaisa for his own
country. A storm arises, and in the height of its fury Thaisa is
delivered of a daughter, who is named Marina because she was
born at sea. The mother swoons and is supposed to be dead. The
sailors insist that she be speedily cast into the sea, in accordance
with their superstition that this alone would allay the tempest.
She is therefore placed in a box by her grief-stricken husband

and consigned to the deep. The box is cast ashore at Ephesus, where those who open it find the lady still alive. Upon recovering strength she becomes a priestess of Diana. Meanwhile Pericles entrusts the infant Marina to Cleon, the governor of Tarsus, and his wife, to be reared by them, and then the Prince proceeds on his way to Tyre.

ACT IV

For fourteen years Marina lives with her guardians at Tarsus, developing into a maiden whose beauty and accomplishments overshadow those of their own daughter. Cleon's jealous wife endeavours to have Marina murdered, but the girl is seized by pirates and conveyed to Mytilene. Here she falls into evil hands, but succeeds in preserving her innocence. In the meantime Pericles visits Tarsus, and is given to understand that his daughter is dead.

ACT V

Overcome with sorrow at the loss of both wife and daughter, Pericles sets sail again for Tyre, but is driven before the winds to Mytilene, where Lysimachus, the governor, pays him a visit on shipboard, but finds him unresponsive and listless. To cheer him, the governor sends for Marina, who had become noted for singing and dancing. She is recognised by her delighted father; and the cup of his happiness is filled to the brim when, shortly afterwards, while on a pilgrimage to Diana's shrine at Ephesus, he is reunited to his long-lost wife Thaisa. He gives his daughter's hand to Lysimachus, while the false Cleon and his wife perish at the hands of incensed citizens of Tarsus.

NOTES

The question of doubtful authorship arises when considering the date of *Pericles*. During Shakespeare's life the play appeared with his name on the title-page, and it was elsewhere ascribed to him; but the authoritative First Folio did not include it. The Quarto appeared in 1609, and in all likelihood the play was written in 1607 or 1608.

FIRST EDITIONS.   As mentioned, a Quarto edition of this play bearing Shakespeare's name was published in 1609. A Second Quarto appeared the same year; a Third, in 1611; a Fourth, in 1619; a Fifth, in 1630; and a Sixth, in 1635. But the First Folio, of 1623, did not include it.

SOURCES.   An ancient Latin tale, "Apollonius Tyrius," is the earliest source of *Pericles*. This Latin story was translated into Saxon and French, among other tongues. More direct sources were Laurence Twine's story, "Pattern of Painful Adventures" (1576); and John Gower's poem, "Confessio Amantis"—the last named being the most direct source of *Pericles*. Gower's name, in fact, is used as the "Chorus" or introducer of the play.

ACTION.   The action extends over a period of about sixteen years. The actual time represented on the stage is fourteen days, the Chorus mentioning the longer intervals.

SELECTED CRITICISM.   "I do not recollect a single plot of Shakespeare's formation in which the majority of the characters are not so well connected, and so necessary in respect of each other, that they proceed in combination to the end of the story; unless the story . . . requires the interposition of death. In *Pericles* this continuity is wanting, and even with the aid of Gower the scenes are rather loosely tacked together than closely interwoven."—STEEVENS.

INDEX TO CHARACTERS

INDEX TO CHARACTERS

✤ ✤ ✤

AARON	*Titus*	ANTIOCHUS	*Pericles*
ABBOT OF WESTMINSTER	*Rich. II*	ANTIPHOLUS OF E.	*Comedy*
ABERGAVENNY, LORD	*Henry VIII*	ANTIPHOLUS OF S.	*Comedy*
ABHORSON	*Measure*	ANTONIO	*Merchant*
ABRAHAM	*Romeo*	ANTONIO	*Much A.*
ACHILLES	*Troilus*	ANTONIO	*Twelfth*
ADAM	*As You*	ANTONIO	*Verona*
ADRIAN	*Tempest*	ANTONIO	*Tempest*
ADRIANA	*Comedy*	ANTONY, MARK	{ *Julius*
ÆGEON	*Comedy*		*Antony*
ÆMILIA	*Comedy*	APEMANTUS	*Timon*
ÆMILIUS	*Titus*	ARCHIBALD	*Henry IV*
ÆNEAS	*Troilus*	ARCHIDAMUS	*Winter's*
AGAMEMNON	*Troilus*	ARIEL	*Tempest* ✓
AGRIPPA	*Antony*	ARMADA, DON A. DE	*Love's*
AGRIPPA, MENENIUS	*Coriol.*	ARTEMIDORUS	*Julius*
AGUECHEEK, SIR ANDREW	*Twelfth*	ARTHUR	*John*
AJAX	*Troilus*	ARVIRAGUS	*Cymbel.*
ALARBUS	*Titus*	AUDREY	*As You*
ALBANY, DUKE OF	*Lear*	AUFIDIUS, TULLUS	*Coriol.*
ALCIBIADES	*Timon*	AUMERLE, DUKE OF	*Rich. II*
ALENÇON, DUKE OF	*Henry VI*	AUTOLYCUS	*Winter's*
ALEXANDER	*Troilus*	AUVERGNE, COUNTESS	
ALEXAS	*Antony*	OF	*Henry VI*
ALICE	*Henry V*		
ALONSO	*Tempest*	BAGOT	*Rich. II*
AMIENS	*As You*	BALTHASAR	*Merchant*
ANDROMACHE	*Troilus*	BALTHASAR	*Much A.*
ANDRONICUS, MARCUS	*Titus*	BALTHASAR	*Romeo*
ANDRONICUS, TITUS	*Titus*	BALTHAZAR	*Comedy*
ANGELO	*Comedy*	BANQUO	*Macbeth*
ANGELO	*Measure*	BAPTISTA	*Taming*
ANGUS	*Macbeth*		{ *Henry IV*
ANNE, LADY	*Rich. III*	BARDOLPH	*Henry V*
ANTENOR	*Troilus*		*Windsor*
ANTIGONUS	*Winter's*	BARNARDINE	*Measure*

BASSANIO	*Merchant*
BASSET	*Henry VI*
BASSIANUS	*Titus*
BATES	*Henry V*
BEATRICE	*Much A.*
BEAUFORT, HENRY	*Henry VI*
BEAUFORT, JOHN	*Henry VI*
BEAUFORT, THOMAS	*Henry VI*
BEDFORD, DUKE OF	{ *Henry V* / *Henry VI*
BELARIUS	*Cymbel.*
BELCH, SIR TOBY	*Twelfth*
BENEDICT	*Much A.*
BENVOLIO	*Romeo*
BERKELEY	{ *Rich. II* / *Rich. III*
BERNARDO	*Hamlet*
BERTRAM	*All's W.*
BEVIS, GEORGE	*Henry VI*
BIANCA	*Othello*
BIANCA	*Taming*
BIGOT, ROBERT	*John*
BIONDELLO	*Taming*
BIRON	*Love's*
BISHOP OF CARLISLE	*Rich. II*
BLANCHE	*John*
BLOUNT, SIR JAMES	*Rich. III*
BLUNT, SIR WALTER	*Henry IV*
BOLINGBROKE, HENRY	*Rich. II*
BOLINGBROKE, ROGER	*Henry VI*
BONA	*Henry VI*
BORACHIO	*Much A.*
BOTTOM	*Midsum.*
BOULT	*Pericles*
BOURBON, DUKE OF	*Henry V*
BOYET	*Love's*
BRABANTIO	*Othello*
BRAKENBURY, SIR ROBT.	*Rich. III*
BRANDON	*Henry VIII*
BRUTUS, DECIUS	*Julius*
BRUTUS, JUNIUS	*Coriol.*
BRUTUS, MARCUS	*Julius*
BUCKINGHAM, DUKE OF	{ *Rich. III* / *Henry VI* / *Henry VIII*
BULLCALF	*Henry IV*
BULLEN, ANNE	*Henry VIII*
BURGH, H. DE	*John*
BURGUNDY, DUKE OF	{ *Henry V* / *Henry VI* / *Lear*
BUSHY	*Rich. II*
BUTTS, DR.	*Henry VIII*
CADE, JACK	*Henry VI*
CÆSAR, JULIUS	*Julius*
CÆSAR, OCTAVIUS	{ *Julius* / *Antony*
CAITHNESS	*Macbeth*
CAIUS	*Titus*
CAIUS, DR.	*Windsor*
CALCHAS	*Troilus*
CALIBAN	*Tempest*
CALPURNIA	*Julius*
CAMBRIDGE, EARL OF	*Henry V*
CAMILLO	*Winter's*
CAMPEIUS, CARDINAL	*Henry VIII*
CANIDIUS	*Antony*
CANTERBURY, ARCH-BISHOP OF	{ *Rich. III* / *Henry V*
CAPHIS	*Timon*
CAPUCIUS	*Henry VIII*
CAPULET	*Romeo*
CAPULET, LADY	*Romeo*
CASCA	*Julius*
CASSANDRA	*Troilus*
CASSIO	*Othello*
CASSIUS	*Julius*
CATESBY, SIR WM.	*Rich. III*
CATO, YOUNG	*Julius*
CELIA	*As You*
CERES	*Tempest*

CERIMON	*Pericles*	CRESSIDA	*Troilus*
CHARLES	*As You*	CROMWELL	*Henry VIII*
CHARLES, THE DAUPHIN	*Henry VI*	CURAN	*Lear*
CHARLES VI, KING	*Henry V*	CURIO	*Twelfth*
CHARMIAN	*Antony*	CURTIS	*Taming*
CHATILLON	*John*	CYMBELINE	*Cymbel.*
CHIRON	*Titus*		
CICERO	*Julius*	DARDANIUS	*Julius*
CIMBER, METELLUS	*Julius*	DAVY	*Henry IV*
CINNA	*Julius*	DEIPHOBUS	*Troilus*
CINNA, A POET	*Julius*	DEMETRIUS	*Antony*
CLARENCE, DUKE OF	*Henry IV*	DEMETRIUS	*Midsum.*
CLARENCE, DUKE OF	*Henry VI*	DEMETRIUS	*Titus*
CLARENCE, DUKE OF	*Rich. III*	DENNIS	*As You*
CLAUDIO	*Measure*	DENNY, SIR AN-	
CLAUDIO	*Much A.*	THONY	*Henry VIII*
CLAUDIUS	*Julius*	DERCETAS	*Antony*
CLAUDIUS	*Hamlet*	DESDEMONA	*Othello*
CLEOMENES	*Winter's*	DIANA	*All's W.*
CLEON	*Pericles*	DICK	*Henry VI*
CLEOPATRA	*Antony*	DIOMEDES	*Antony*
CLIFFORD, LORD	*Henry VI*	DIOMEDES	*Troilus*
CLIFFORD, YOUNG	*Henry VI*	DION	*Winter's*
CLITUS	*Julius*	DIONYZA	*Pericles*
CLOTEN	*Cymbel.*	DOGBERRY	*Much A.*
COBWEB	*Midsum.*	DOLABELLA	*Antony*
COLVILLE, SIR JOHN	*Henry IV*	DONALBAIN	*Macbeth*
COMINIUS	*Coriol.*	DON JOHN	*Much A.*
CONRADE	*Much A.*	DON PEDRO	*Much A.*
CONSTANCE	*John*	DORCAS	*Winter's*
CORDELIA	*Lear*	DORSET, MARQUIS OF	*Rich. III*
CORIN	*As You*	DROMIO OF E.	*Comedy*
CORIOLANUS (CAIUS MAR-		DROMIO OF S.	*Comedy*
CIUS)	*Coriol.*	DUKE	*As You*
CORNELIUS	*Cymbel.*	DULL	*Love's*
CORNELIUS	*Hamlet*	DUMAIN	*Love's*
CORNWALL, DUKE OF	*Hamlet*	DUNCAN	*Macbeth*
COSTARD	*Love's*		
COUNTESS OF ROUSILLON	*All's W.*	EDGAR	*Lear*
COURT	*Henry V*	EDMUND	*Lear*
CRANMER	*Henry VIII*	EDMUND OF LANGLEY	*Rich. II*

EDWARD	*Henry VI*
EDWARD, PRINCE	*Rich. III*
EDWARD IV, KING	*Rich. III*
EGEUS	*Midsum.*
EGLAMOUR	*Verona*
ELBOW	*Measure*
ELINOR, QUEEN	*John*
ELIZABETH, QUEEN	*Rich. III*
ELY, BISHOP OF	{ *Henry V* / *Rich. III* }
EMILIA	*Othello*
EMILIA	*Winter's*
ENOBARBUS, DOMITIUS	*Antony*
EROS	*Antony*
ERPINGHAM, SIR THOS.	*Henry V*
ESCALUS	*Measure*
ESCALUS	*Romeo*
ESCANES	*Pericles*
EUPHRONIUS	*Antony*
EVANS, SIR HUGH	*Windsor*
EXETER, DUKE OF	{ *Henry V* / *Henry VI* }
FABIAN	*Twelfth*
FALSTAFF, SIR JOHN	{ *Windsor* / *Henry IV* }
FANG	*Henry IV*
FASTOLFE, SIR JOHN	*Henry VI*
FAULCONBRIDGE, LADY	*John*
FAULCONBRIDGE, ROBERT	*John*
FEEBLE	*Henry IV*
FENTON	*Windsor*
FERDINAND	*Love's*
FERDINAND	*Tempest*
FESTE	*Twelfth*
FITZ-PETER, GEFFREY	*John*
FITZWALTER, LORD	*Rich. II*
FLAMINIUS	*Timon*
FLAVIUS	*Julius*
FLAVIUS	*Timon*
FLEANCE	*Macbeth*
FLORENCE, DUKE OF	*All's W.*
FLORIZEL	*Winter's*
FLUELLEN	*Henry V*
FLUTE	*Midsum.*
FORD	*Windsor*
FORD, MISTRESS	*Windsor*
FORTINBRAS	*Hamlet*
FRANCIS, FRIAR	*Much A.*
FRANCISCA	*Measure*
FRANCISCO	*Hamlet*
FRANCISCO	*Tempest*
FREDERICK	*As You*
FROTH	*Measure*
GADSHILL	*Henry IV*
GALLUS	*Antony*
GARDINER	*Henry VIII*
GARGRAVE, SIR THOS.	*Henry VI*
GERTRUDE	*Hamlet*
GLANSDALE, SIR WM.	*Henry VI*
GLENDOWER, OWEN	*Henry IV*
GLOUCESTER, DUCHESS OF	*Rich. II*
GLOUCESTER, DUKE OF	*Henry V*
GLOUCESTER, DUKE OF	*Henry VI*
GLOUCESTER, DUKE OF	*Rich. III*
GLOUCESTER, EARL OF	*Lear*
GOBBO, LAUNCELOT	*Merchant*
GOBBO, OLD	*Merchant*
GOFFE, MATTHEW	*Henry VI*
GONERIL	*Lear*
GONZALO	*Tempest*
GOWER	{ *Henry IV* / *Henry V* }
GOWER	*Pericles*
GRANDPRÉ	*Henry V*
GRATIANO	*Merchant*
GRATIANO	*Othello*
GREEN	*Rich. II*
GREGORY	*Romeo*
GREMIO	*Taming*
GREY, LADY ELIZABETH	*Henry VI*

GREY, LORD	*Rich. III*	HOTSPUR	⎰ *Henry IV*
GREY, SIR THOS.	*Henry V*	(HENRY PERCY)	⎱ *Rich. II*
GRIFFITH	*Henry VIII*	HUME, JOHN	*Henry VI*
GRUMIO	*Taming*	HUMPHREY OF GLOS-	⎰ *Henry IV*
GUIDERIUS	*Cymbel.*	TER	⎱ *Henry VI*
GUILDENSTERN	*Hamlet*		
GUILDFORD, SIR HENRY		IACHIMO	*Cymbel.*
	Henry VIII	IAGO	*Othello*
GURNEY, JAMES	*John*	IDEN, ALEX	*Henry VI*
		IMOGEN	*Cymbel.*
		IRAS	*Antony*
		IRIS	*Tempest*
HAMLET	*Hamlet*	ISABEL, QUEEN	*Henry V*
HARCOURT	*Henry IV*	ISABELLA	*Measure*
HASTINGS, LORD	*Henry IV*		
HASTINGS, LORD	*Henry VI*		
HASTINGS, LORD	*Rich. III*	JAMY	*Henry V*
HECATE	*Macbeth*	JAQUENETTA	*Love's*
HECTOR	*Troilus*	JAQUES	*As You*
HELEN	*Cymbel.*	JESSICA	*Merchant*
HELEN	*Troilus*	JOAN LA PUCELLE	*Henry VI*
HELENA	*All's W.*	JOHN, FRIAR	*Romeo*
HELENA	*Midsum.*	JOHN, KING	*John*
HELENUS	*Troilus*	JOHN OF GAUNT	*Rich. II*
HELICANUS	*Pericles*	JOHN OF LANCASTER	*Henry IV*
HENRY, PRINCE	*Henry IV*	JOURDAIN, MARGARET	*Henry VI*
HENRY, PRINCE	*John*	JULIA	*Verona*
HENRY IV, KING	*Henry IV*	JULIET	*Measure*
HENRY V, KING	*Henry V*	JULIET	*Romeo*
HENRY VI, KING	*Henry VI*	JUNO	*Tempest*
HENRY VIII, KING	*Henry VIII*		
HERBERT, SIR WALTER	*Rich. III*	KATHARINA	*Taming*
HERMIA	*Midsum.*	KATHARINE	*Henry V*
HERMIONE	*Winter's*	KATHARINE	*Love's*
HERO	*Much A.*	KATHARINE, QUEEN	*Henry VIII*
HIPPOLYTA	*Midsum.*	KENT, EARL OF	*Lear*
HOLLAND, JOHN	*Henry VI*	KING OF FRANCE	*All's W.*
HOLOFERNES	*Love's*	KING OF FRANCE	*Lear*
HORATIO	*Hamlet*		
HORNER, THOS.	*Henry VI*	LAERTES	*Hamlet*
HORTENSIO	*Taming*	LAFEU	*All's W.*
HORTENSIUS	*Timon*	LARTIUS, TITUS	*Coriol.*

LAUNCE	*Verona*
LAURENCE, FRIAR	*Romeo*
LAVACHE	*All's W.*
LAVINIA	*Titus*
LEAR, KING	*Lear*
LE BEAU	*As You*
LEGARIUS	*Julius*
LENA, POPILIUS	*Julius*
LENNOX	*Macbeth*
LEONARDO	*Merchant*
LEONATO	*Much A.*
LEONATUS, POSTHUMUS	*Cymbel.*
LEONINE	*Pericles*
LEONTES	*Winter's*
LEPIDUS M. ÆMILIUS	{ *Antony* / *Julius*
LEWIS	*John*
LEWIS, THE DAUPHIN	*Henry V*
LEWIS XI, KING	*Henry VI*
LIMOGES, DUKE	*John*
LINCOLN, BISHOP OF	*Henry VIII*
LODOVICO	*Othello*
LONGAVILLE	*Love's*
LONGSWORD, WILLIAM	*John*
LORENZO	*Merchant*
LOVEL, LORD	*Rich. III*
LOVELL, SIR THOS.	*Henry VIII*
LUCE	*Comedy*
LUCENTIO	*Taming*
LUCETTA	*Verona*
LUCIANA	*Comedy*
LUCILIUS	*Julius*
LUCILIUS	*Timon*
LUCIO	*Measure*
LUCIUS	*Julius*
LUCIUS	*Timon*
LUCIUS	*Titus*
LUCIUS, CAIUS	*Cymbel.*
LUCIUS, YOUNG	*Titus*
LUCULLUS	*Timon*
LUCY, SIR WM.	*Henry VI*
LYCHORIDA	*Pericles*
LYSANDER	*Midsum.*
LYSIMACHUS	*Pericles*
MACBETH	*Macbeth*
MACBETH, LADY	*Macbeth*
MACDUFF	*Macbeth*
MACDUFF, LADY	*Macbeth*
MACMORRIS	*Henry V*
MALCOLM	*Macbeth*
MALVOLIO	*Twelfth*
MANILLIUS	*Winter's*
MARCELLUS	*Hamlet*
MARCH, EARL OF	*Henry VI*
MARDIAN	*Antony*
MARESHALL, WILLIAM	*John*
MARGARELON	*Troilus*
MARGARET	*Henry VI*
MARGARET	*Much A.*
MARGARET, QUEEN	{ *Henry VI* / *Rich. III*
MARIA	*Love's*
MARIA	*Twelfth*
MARIANA	*All's W.*
MARIANNA	*Measure*
MARINA	*Pericles*
MARSHAL, LORD	*Rich. II*
MARTEXT, SIR OLIVER	*As You*
MARTIUS	*Coriol.*
MARTIUS	*Titus*
MARULLUS	*Julius*
MECÆNAS	*Antony*
MELUN	*John*
MENAS	*Antony*
MENECRATES	*Antony*
MENELAUS	*Troilus*
MENTEITH	*Macbeth*
MERCADE	*Love's*
MERCUTIO	*Romeo*
MESSALA	*Julius*
MICHAEL	*Henry VI*

MICHAEL, SIR	*Henry IV*	OLIVER	*As You*	
MILAN, DUKE OF	*Verona*	OLIVIA	*Twelfth*	
MIRANDA	*Tempest*	OPHELIA	*Hamlet*	
MONTAGUE	*Romeo*	ORLANDO	*As You*	
MONTAGUE, LADY	*Romeo*	ORLEANS, BASTARD OF	*Henry VI*	
MONTAGUE, MARQUESS		ORLEANS, DUKE OF	*Henry V*	
OF	*Henry VI*	ORSINO	*Twelfth*	
MONTANO	*Othello*	OSRIC	*Hamlet*	
MONTGOMERY, SIR		OSWALD	*Lear*	
JOHN	*Henry VI*	OTHELLO	*Othello*	
MONTJOY	*Henry V*	OVERDONE, MRS.	*Measure*	
MOPSA	*Winter's*	OXFORD, EARL OF	{ *Henry VI* *Rich. III*	
MORTIMER, EDMUND	{ *Henry IV* *Henry VI*			
MORTIMER, SIR HUGH	*Henry VI*	PAGE	*Windsor*	
MORTIMER, SIR JOHN	*Henry VI*	PAGE, ANNE	*Windsor*	
MORTIMER, LADY	*Henry IV*	PAGE, MISTRESS	*Windsor*	
MORTON	*Henry IV*	PAGE, WILLIAM	*Windsor*	
MOTH	*Love's*	PANDARUS	*Troilus*	
MOTH	*Midsum.*	PANDOLPH, CARDINAL	*John*	
MOULDY	*Henry IV*	PANTHINO	*Verona*	
MOWBRAY, THOMAS	*Rich. II*	PARIS	*Romeo*	
MUSTARDSEED	*Midsum.*	PARIS	*Troilus*	
MUTIUS	*Titus*	PAROLLES	*All's W.*	
		PATIENCE	*Henry VIII*	
NATHANIEL, SIR	*Love's*	PATROCLUS	*Troilus*	
NERISSA	*Merchant*	PAULINA	*Winter's*	
NESTOR	*Troilus*	PEASEBLOSSOM	*Midsum.*	
NORFOLK, DUKE OF	{ *Henry VI* *Rich. III*	PEMBROKE, EARL OF	*Henry VI*	
NORFOLK, DUKE OF	*Henry VIII*	PERCY, HENRY	{ *Rich. II* *Henry IV*	
NORTHUMBERLAND, EARL OF	{ *Henry IV* *Henry VI* *Rich. II*	PERCY, LADY	*Henry IV*	
		PERCY, THOS.	*Henry IV*	
		PERDITA	*Winter's*	
NORTHUMBERLAND, LADY	*Henry IV*	PERICLES	*Pericles*	
		PETER	*Henry VI*	
NYM	{ *Windsor* *Henry V*	PETER	*Measure*	
		PETER	*Romeo*	
		PETER OF POMFRET	*John*	
OBERON	*Midsum.*	PETO	*Henry IV*	
OCTAVIA	*Antony*	PETRUCHIO	*Taming*	

PHEBE	*As You*
PHILARO	*Cymbel.*
PHILEMON	*Pericles*
PHILIP	*John*
PHILIP, KING	*John*
PHILO	*Antony*
PHILOSTRATE	*Midsum.*
PHILOTUS	*Timon*
PHRYNIA	*Timon*
PIERCE OF EXTON, SIR	*Rich. II*
PINCH	*Comedy*
PINDARUS	*Julius*
PISANIO	*Cymbel.*
PISTOL	*Henry IV* / *Henry V* / *Windsor*
PLANTAGENET, MAR-GARET	*Rich. III*
PLANTAGENET, RICHARD	*Henry VI*
POINS	*Henry IV*
POLIXENES	*Winter's*
POLONIUS	*Hamlet*
POMPEIUS, SEXTUS	*Antony*
POMPEY	*Measure*
PORTIA	*Julius*
PORTIA	*Merchant*
PRIAM	*Troilus*
PRINCE OF ARRAGON	*Merchant*
PRINCE OF MOROCCO	*Merchant*
PROCULEIUS	*Antony*
PROSPERO	*Tempest*
PROTEUS	*Verona*
PUBLIUS	*Julius*
PUBLIUS	*Titus*
PUCK	*Midsum.*
QUICKLY	*Windsor*
QUICKLY, MRS.	*Henry IV* / *Henry V*
QUINCE	*Midsum.*
QUINTUS	*Titus*
RAMBURES	*Henry V*
RATCLIFF, SIR RICH.	*Rich. III*
REGAN	*Lear*
REIGNIER, DUKE OF ANJOU	*Henry VI*
REYNALDO	*Hamlet*
RICHARD	*Henry VI*
RICHARD II, KING	*Rich. II*
RICHARD III, KING	*Rich. III*
RICHMOND, EARL OF	*Henry VI* / *Rich. III*
RIVERS, LORD	*Henry VI* / *Rich. III*
ROBIN	*Windsor*
RODERIGO	*Othello*
ROGERO	*Winter's*
ROMEO	*Romeo*
ROSALIND	*As You*
ROSALINE	*Love's*
ROSENCRANTZ	*Hamlet*
ROSS	*Macbeth*
ROSS, LORD	*Rich. II*
RUGBY	*Windsor*
RUMOUR	*Henry IV*
RUTLAND, EARL OF	*Henry VI*
SALARINO	*Merchant*
SALERIO	*Merchant*
SALISBURY, EARL OF	*Henry V* / *Henry VI* / *Rich. II*
SAMPSON	*Romeo*
SANDS, LORD	*Henry VIII*
SATURNINUS	*Titus*
SAY, LORD	*Henry VI*
SCALES, LORD	*Henry VI*
SCARUS	*Antony*
SCROOP, RICHARD	*Henry IV* / *Henry V*
SCROOP, SIR STEPHEN	*Rich. II*
SEBASTIAN	*Tempest*

SEBASTIAN	*Twelfth*	SUFFOLK, EARL OF	*Henry VI*
SELEUCUS	*Antony*	SUFFOLK, EARL OF	*Henry VIII*
SEMPRONIUS	*Timon*	SURREY, DUKE OF	*Rich. II*
SEMPRONIUS	*Titus*	SURREY, EARL OF	*Henry IV*
SERVILIUS	*Timon*	SURREY, EARL OF	*Henry VIII*
SEYTON	*Macbeth*	SURREY, EARL OF	*Rich. III*
SHADOW	*Henry IV*		
SHALLOW	*{ Windsor*	TALBOT, JOHN	*Henry VI*
	{ Henry IV	TALBOT, LORD	*Henry VI*
SHYLOCK	*Merchant*	TAMORA	*Titus*
SILANIO	*Merchant*	TAURUS	*Antony*
SILENCE	*Henry VI*	TEARSHEET, DOLL	*Henry IV*
SILIUS	*Antony*	THAISA	*Pericles*
SILVIA	*Verona*	THALIARD	*Pericles*
SILVIUS	*As You*	THERSITES	*Troilus*
SIMONIDES	*Pericles*	THESEUS	*Midsum.*
SIMPCOX	*Henry VI*	THOMAS	*Measure*
SIMPLE	*Windsor*	THURIO	*Verona*
SIWARD	*Macbeth*	THYREUS	*Antony*
SIWARD, YOUNG	*Macbeth*	TIMANDRA	*Timon*
SLENDER	*Windsor*	TIMON	*Timon*
SLY, CHRISTOPHER	*Taming*	TITANIA	*Midsum.*
SMITH	*Henry VI*	TITINIUS	*Julius*
SNARE	*Henry IV*	TITUS	*Timon*
SNOUT	*Midsum.*	TOUCHSTONE	*As You*
SNUG	*Midsum.*	TRAVERS	*Henry IV*
SOLINUS	*Comedy*	TREBONIUS	*Julius*
SOMERSET, DUKE OF	*Henry VI*	TRESSEL	*Rich. III*
SOMERVILLE, SIR JOHN	*Henry VI*	TRINCULO	*Tempest*
SOUTHWELL, JOHN	*Henry VI*	TROILUS	*Troilus*
SPEED	*Verona*	TUBAL	*Merchant*
STAFFORD, SIR HUM-		TYBALT	*Romeo*
PHREY	*Henry VI*	TYRREL, SIR JAMES	*Rich. III*
STAFFORD, WILLIAM	*Henry VI*		
STANLEY, LORD	*Rich. III*	ULYSSES	*Troilus*
STANLEY, SIR JOHN	*Henry VI*	URSULA	*Much A.*
STANLEY, SIR WM.	*Henry VI*	URSWICK, CHRISTOPHER	*Rich. III*
STARVELING	*Midsum.*		
STEPHANO	*Merchant*	VALENTINE	*Titus*
STEPHANO	*Tempest*	VALENTINE	*Twelfth*
STRATO	*Julius*	VALENTINE	*Verona*

VALERIA	*Coriol.*	VOLUMNIA	*Coriol.*
VARRIUS	*Antony*	VOLUMNIUS	*Julius*
VARRIUS	*Measure*	WART	*Henry IV*
VARRO	*Julius*		
VAUGHAN, SIR THOS.	*Rich. III*	WARWICK, EARL OF $\left\{\begin{array}{l} Henry\ IV \\ Henry\ V \\ Henry\ VI \end{array}\right.$	
VAUX	*Henry VI*		
VAUX, SIR NICHOLAS	*Henry VIII*		
VELUTUS, CINIUS	*Coriol.*	WESTMORELAND, EARL OF $\left\{\begin{array}{l} Henry\ IV \\ Henry\ V \\ Henry\ VI \end{array}\right.$	
VENICE, DUKE OF	*Merchant*		
VENICE, DUKE OF	*Othello*	WHITMORE, WALTER	*Henry VI*
VENTIDIUS	*Antony*	WILLIAM	*As You*
VENTIDIUS	*Timon*	WILLIAMS	*Henry V*
VERGES	*Much A.*	WILLOUGHBY	*Rich. II*
VERGILIA	*Coriol.*	WOLSEY, CARDINAL	*Henry VIII*
VERNON	*Henry VI*	WOODVILLE	*Henry VI*
VERNON, SIR RICHARD	*Henry IV*		
VINCENTIO	*Measure*	YORK, ARCHBISHOP OF	*Rich. III*
VINCENTIO	*Taming*	YORK, DUCHESS OF	*Rich. II*
VIOLA	*Twelfth*	YORK, DUCHESS OF	*Rich. III*
VIOLENTA	*All's W.*	YORK, DUKE OF	*Henry V*
VOLTIMAND	*Hamlet*	YORK, DUKE OF	*Rich. III*